SWU-800- 003

UNIFORMS OF RUSSIAN ARMY DURING THE YEARS 1825-1855 VOL. 3

UNDER THE REIGN OF NICHOLAS I
EMPEROR OF RUSSIA BETWEEN 1825 TO 1855
CAVALRY: DRAGOONS,HORSE-JAGERS,LANCERS & HUSSARS

From the Viskovatov's greatest work:
"Historical description of the clothing and
arms of the Russian Army"

English translation by Mark Conrad

SOLDIERSHOP PUBLISHING

AUTHOR

Aleksandr Vasilevich Viskovatov born 22 April (4 May New Style) 1804, died 27 February (11 March) 1858 in St. Petersburg, Russian military historian. He graduated from the 1st Cadet Corps and served in the artillery, the hydrographic depot of the Naval Ministry, and then in the Department of Military Educational Institutions. He mainly studied historical artifacts and the histories of military units. Viskovatov's greatest work was the Historical Description of the Clothing and Arms of the Russian Army.

Title: **UNIFORMS OF RUSSIAN ARMY IN THE XVIII Cent. VOL. 3 -**
The Russian Army under the reign of Catherine the Great 1762-1796
By A.V.Viskovatov. Serie edit by Luca S. Cristini. First edition by Soldiershop. July 2017
Cover & Art Design: Luca S. Cristini. Plates re-colorations by Anna Cristini.
ISBN code: 978-88-93272612
Published by Soldiershop publishing, via Padre Davide, 7 - 24050 Zanica (BG) ITALY. www.soldiershop.com

UNIFORMS
OF THE RUSSIAN ARMY
DURING THE YEARS
1825-1855
VOL. 3

UNDER THE REIGN OF NICHOLAS I EMPEROUR OF
RUSSIA BETWEEN 1825 AND 1855

Portrait of Grand Duke Nicholas, later Emperor Nicholas I (1825-55, on horseback by George Dawe (c.1820,)

HISTORICAL DESCRIPTION OF THE CLOTHING AND ARMS OF THE RUSSIAN ARMY - A.V. VISKOVATOV
(First English translation by Mark Conrad)

Soldiershop is glad to presents the complete collection of the great job made by A.V. Viskovatov dedicated to the uniforms and weapons belonging from the first Zar and Russian emperors to the Russian army during the Napoleonic period, until 1860 about. The time we considered in this volume corresponds to the reigns of Catherine the Great (Catherine II) who reigned since 1762 until his murder on the 6 November 1796.

Our reprint in based on the original 19th century volumes, to be precise the volumes from 4 to 6 are dedicated to the reign of Catherine II; this part is distributed on 3 or 4 volumes.

Our new edition, the first ever published in English, both on paper and digital format, boasts a large number of color plates, many of them unpublished and re-coloured by our team of expert artists and scholars of uniformology. Each volume is based on 100 color plates or more, always accompanied by the original translated text which describes the subjets of the plates.

A unique work in its genre, a must have in any respecting collection!

Aleksandr Vasilevich Viskovatov born 22 April (4 May New Style) 1804, died 27 February (11 March) 1858 in St. Petersburg, Russian military historian. He graduated from the 1st Cadet Corps and served in the artillery, the hydrographic depot of the Naval Ministry, and then in the Department of Military Educational Institutions.

He mainly studied historical artifacts and the histories of military units. Viskovatov's greatest work was the Historical Description of the Clothing and Arms of the Russian Army (Vols. 1-30, St. Petersburg, 1841-62; 2nd ed. Vols. 1-34, St. Petersburg - Novosibirsk - Leningrad, 1899-1948). This work is based on a great quantity of archival documents and contains four thousand colored illustrations.

Viskovatov was the author of Chronicles of the Russian Army (Books 1-20, St. Petersburg, 1834-42) and Chronicles of the Russian Imperial Army (Parts 1-7, St. Petersburg, 1852). He collected valuable material on the history of the Russian navy which went into A Short Overview of Russian Naval Campaigns and General Voyages to the End of the XVII Century (St. Petersburg, 1864; 2nd edition Moscow, 1946). Together with A.I. Mikhailovskii-Danilevskii he helped prepare and create the Military Gallery in the Winter Palace.

He wrote the historical military inscriptions for the walls of the Hall of St. George in the Great Palace of the Kremlin. (From the article in the Soviet Military Encyclopedia.)

CONTENTS

*

Preface pag. 5

*

HISTORICAL DESCRIPTION OF THE CLOTHING AND ARMS OF THE RUSSIAN ARMY
Dragoons, Horse-Jagers, Lancers & Hussars

CHANGES IN THE UNIFORM AND ARMS OF THE ARMY FROM 20 NOVEMBER, 1825, TO 18 FEBRUARY, 1855:

7. DRAGOON REGIMENTS (DRAGUNSKIE POLKI).

11 February 1826 - Clerks [*pisarya*] and in general all lower ranks are ordered to have grey **riding trousers** [*reituzy*] with stripes [*lampasy*] [1].

10 June 1826 - Instead of the dark-green pants [*pantalony*] with stripes, it is ordered that grey cloth **riding trousers** without stripes always be worn, with piping on the side seam according to the color of the collar (Illus. 213, 214, 215, 216, 217, 218, 219, 220, and 221) [2].

15 September 1826 - Lower ranks who have served out the regulation number of years without reproach and who voluntarily remain on service are ordered to wear **gold galloon** [*nashivka iz zolotago galuna*] sewn onto the left sleeve, as related above for Grenadier regiments [3].

1 January 1827 - In order to distinguish **rank**, it is ordered that officers' epaulettes are to have small forged and stamped stars of the same appearance and according to the same scheme as related above for Grenadier regiments [4].

31 July 1827 - Numbers and letters on **shako covers** [*kivernye chekhly*] are directed to be in yellow oil paints [5].

8 October 1827 - A new pattern of **saber** [*sablya*] is confirmed, with a brass hilt [*yefes*], black grip [*grif*], and iron scabbard [*nozhny*], straighter than previously [6].

13 October 1827 - In place of the fringed woollen **epaulettes** [*epolety*] on their coats, lower ranks are given scaled [*cheshuichatyi*] ones without fringes, the same color as the buttons, with a cloth backing and small cross-strap [*pogonchik*] the same color as the collar (Illus. 223). Along with this, the fields of officers' epaulettes are also ordered to be scaled (Illus. 224) [7].

10 November 1827 - The following Dragoon regiments are ordered to have the indicated **colors** for: collars, cuffs, cuff flaps, lining to skirts and turnbacks of the coat [*mundir*]: Moscow - orange (Illus. 225); Kargopol - white (Illus. 225); Kinburn - turquoise [*biryuzovyi*] (Illus. 226); New Russia [*Novorossiiskii*] - rose [*rozovyi*] (Illus. 226); Kazan - raspberry [*malinovyi*] (Illus. 226); His Royal Highness Duke Alexander of Württemberg's (formerly the Riga) - red (Illus. 227); Tver - light blue [*svetlosinii*] (Illus. 227); Finland - yellow (Illus. 227); Nizhnii-Novgorod - brick [*kirpichnyi*] (Illus. 227). In all these regiments there is dark-green piping around the collar, cuffs, cuff flaps, and turnbacks. Appointments are brass, but gold for officers [8].

14 December 1827 - The **lace** [*nashivka*] sewn onto lower ranks' left sleeves, instituted on 15 September 1826, is to be gold, of the non-commissioned officers' galloon of the regiment in which a man has served out the regulation period required for discharge yet volunteers to remain on service [9].

9 February 1828 - A new pattern **shako** [*kiver*] is issued, stipulated to have a height of 9 1/2 inches, an upper diameter of not less than 9 3/4 inches and not more than 10 1/2, and a lower diameter according to the size of the head. The width of the upper lacquered edge is 1/2 inch, with a pompon and cords or lines [*vitishkety ili snurok*] in yellow, but in silver for officers. Plates [*gerby*] for these shakos remain as before (Illus. 228, 229, and 230) [10].

7 March 1828 - Lower ranks who return to their regiments from the Model Cavalry Regiment, as well as those who have previously been in the Instructional Cavalry Squadron, are to have **yellow tape** [*bason*] sewn onto the shoulder straps of the greatcoat, of the same appearance and patterns as related above for Grenadier regiments. The same tape is also ordered to be on epaulettes (Illus. 231) [11].

24 April 1828 - Instead of the grey coats [*mundiry serago sveta*] previously used by them, all non-combatant non-commissioned officers throughout are given dark-green **frock coats** with one row of buttons [*temnozelenye, odnobortnye syurtuki*] and the same collar, cuffs, and shoulder straps as for combatants, while the pants are grey with piping on the side seams in the same color as the collar. Instead of their previous coats [*mundiry*], non-combatant master-craftsmen lower ranks [*masterovye nestroevye nizhnie chiny*], as well as infirmary orderlies [*lazaretynye sluzhiteli*], are to wear **jackets** of grey cloth, with distinctions as on the coats [*kurtki serago sukna, po obraztsu mundirov*], while pants are as for the preceding non-combatants [12]

20 December 1828 - A new pattern for the **shako plate** is confirmed based on those established on 24 April 1828 for Infantry and Jäger regiments, with a cut-out figure of the regiment's assigned number (Illus. 232): in the Moscow Regiment - *1*, Kargopol - *2*, Kinburn - *3*, New Russia - *4*, Kazan - *5*, His Royal Highness Duke Alexander of Württemberg's - *6*, Tver - *7*, Finland - *8*, and Nizhnii-Novgorod - *9* [13]

10 August 1829 - The **Nizhnii-Novgorod Dragoon Regiment** is ordered to use sheepskin *shapka* headdresses instead of shakos, of the same pattern as those established at this time for the Infantry of the Separate Caucasus Corps (Illus. 233) [14].

16 December 1829 - The cuffs of officers' **frock coats** [*syurtuki*] are to be the same color as the frock instead of being colored, with piping of the same color as the collar of the coat [*mundir*] [15].

26 December 1829 - All combatant ranks are ordered to have uniform **buttons** with the raised image of the numeral prescribed for the shako plate [16].

6 April 1830 - The Kargopol and New Russia Dragoon Regiments are awarded **shako badges** [*znaki na kivera*] with the inscription: "*Za otlichie*" ["For excellence"], following the model of these same badges in the Army Infantry [17].

22 September 1830 - The same **badges** are awarded to the Nizhnii-Novgorod Dragoon Regiment [18].

24 September 1830 - The lining [*podkladka*] of officers' **frock coats** is to be dark green like the color of the frock coat itself [19].

1 January 1832 - Generals who have **gold swords**, decorated with diamonds and with the inscription "*Za khrabost*" ["For courage"], are to wear these without swordknots [20].

8 September 1832 - All combatant non-commissioned officers are given **muskets** [*ruzhya*] [21].

3 January 1833 - **Covers** for shakos are discontinued [22].

20 January 1833 - **Covers** for shakos are kept as before [23].

22 February 1833 - Field and company-grade officers are not to wear hats, but at all times be in **shakos** [24].

16 March 1833 - **Undress coats** [*vitse-mundiry*] for field and company-grade officers are abolished, with only generals being allowed to wear them [25].

19 March 1833 - **Bandoliers** [*pantalery*] are abolished in all Dragoon regiments, and the hooks that were on them are directed to be put on the cartridge-pouch belt [26].

21 March 1833 - With the reorganization of all Dragoon regiments, except the Nizhnii-Novgorod, to consist of 10 active squadrons and one reserve one, the ninth and tenth, i.e. the Lancer squadrons [*Pikinernye eskadrony*], are not authorized muskets, but rather are prescribed **carbines** and **lances** [*karabiny i piki*]. Along with this the regiments are to have **horses** as follows: *Moscow* — sorrels [*ryzhie*]; *Kargopol* - chestnuts [*gnedye*], and henceforth greys [*serye*]; *Kinburn* — chestnuts; *New Russia* - blacks [*voronye*], with bays [*karie*] and dark chestnuts [*temnognedye*] allowed to be included; *Kazan* — chestnuts; *His Royal Highness Duke Alexander of Württemberg's* — greys; *Tver* - blacks, with bays and dark chestnuts allowed to be included; *Finland* — sorrels [27].

13 April 1833 - In the 9th and 10th squadrons of Dragoon regiments, both ranks [*v obeikh sherengakh*] are ordered to have **carbines** and **lances**, with the first being replaced by horse-jäger muskets without bayonets [*konno-yegerskiya ruzhya, bez shtykov*] until such time as squadrons are able to be supplied with them [28].

5 May 1833 - The numbers on **shako plates** are ordered to be fixed on and not cut out [*ne proreznyi, a nakladnyi*]: for lower ranks made out of tin [*olovo*] and silver-plated [*vyserebryannyi*] for officers, as was introduced at this time for Infantry and Jäger regiments [29].

20 October 1833 - **Pennons** [*flyugera*] for lances are confirmed: in the Moscow Regiment — white with orange tails; in the Kargopol — all white; in the Kinburn — white with turquoise; in the New Russia — white with light blue; in the Kazan — raspberry with white; in the Riga (formerly His Royal Highness Duke Alexander of Württemberg's) — red with white; in the Tver — light blue with white; in the Finland — yellow with white (Illus. 234) [30].

24 December 1833 - The regiments of the 1st and 2nd Dragoon Divisions are ordered to have new **uniforms** as follows:

Finland Regiment	dark-green coat, piping on the collar, on the cuffs, and on the cuff-flaps, and collar patches; light-blue collar, cuffs, lining to the skirts and turnbacks, piping down the front, cuff-flaps, and piping on the riding trousers; small light-blue cross-straps on the epaulettes, with dark-green piping; brass buttons and shako plates, with the numeral *8* (Illus. 239).

Moscow Regiment	dark-green coat, collar, and piping on the cuffs and cuff-flaps; red piping on the collar, collar patches, cuffs, lining to the skirts and turnbacks, piping down the front, cuff-flaps, and piping on the riding trousers; small red cross-straps on the epaulettes, with dark-green piping; brass buttons and shako plates, with the numeral *1* (Illus. 235).
Kargopol Regiment	dark-green coat, collar, and piping on the cuffs and cuff-flaps; white piping on the collar, collar patches, cuffs, lining to the skirts and turnbacks, piping down the front, cuff-flaps, and piping on the riding trousers; small white cross-straps on the epaulettes, with dark-green piping; brass buttons and shako plates, with the numeral *2* (Illus. 235).
Kinburn Regiment	dark-green coat, collar, and piping on the cuffs and cuff-flaps; yellow piping on the collar, collar patches, cuffs, lining to the skirts and turnbacks, piping down the front, cuff-flaps, and piping on the riding trousers; small yellow cross-straps on the epaulettes, with dark-green piping; brass buttons and shako plates, with the numeral *3* (Illus. 236).
New-Russia Regiment	dark-green coat, collar, and piping on the cuffs and cuff-flaps; light-blue piping on the collar, collar patches, cuffs, lining to the skirts and turnbacks, piping down the front, cuff-flaps, and piping on the riding trousers; small light-blue cross-straps on the epaulettes, with dark-green piping; brass buttons and shako plates, with the numeral *4* (Illus. 237).
Kazan Regiment	dark-green coat, piping on the collar, on the cuffs, and on the cuff-flaps, and collar patches; red collar, cuffs, lining to the skirts and turnbacks, piping down the front, cuff-flaps, and piping on the riding trousers; small red cross-straps on the epaulettes, with dark-green piping; brass buttons and shako plates, with the numeral *5* (Illus. 238).
Riga Regiment	dark-green coat, piping on the collar, on the cuffs, and on the cuff-flaps, and collar patches; white collar, cuffs, lining to the skirts and turnbacks, piping down the front, cuff-flaps, and piping on the riding trousers; small white cross-straps on the epaulettes, with dark-green piping; brass buttons and shako plates, with the numeral *6* (Illus. 238).
Tver Regiment	dark-green coat, piping on the collar, on the cuffs, and on the cuff-flaps, and collar patches; yellow collar, cuffs, lining to the skirts and turnbacks, piping down the front, cuff-flaps, and piping on the riding trousers; small yellow cross-straps on the epaulettes, with dark-green piping; brass buttons and shako plates, with the numeral *7* (Illus. 239).

All these regiments are given a lancer-style **girdle** [*ulanskago obraztsa kushaki*], with a dark-green middle and piping, while the edges are the color of the cuffs. **Riding trousers** are greyish-blue [*serosinevatyi*]. **Swordbelts** [*portupei*] are red, of Russian leather [*yuftovaya kozha*] [31].

9 January 1834 - The *Moscow Regiment* is directed to have chestnut **horses**; the *Kinburn* - sorrels. The *Finland Regiment* is to have yellow as the regimental color and the numeral 7 on buttons and shako plates, while the *Tver* - the color light blue and the numeral 8 [32].

6 April 1834 - In Dragoon regiments it is ordered that **muskets** are not to be held in buckets [*bushmaty*], but carried over the shoulder on a strap of the newly confirmed pattern; consequently the buckets on the saddles are discontinued (Illus. 240) [33].

13 April 1834 - **Cartridge pouches** and **crossbelts** are to be of the new pattern, with smaller-sized cover flaps and narrower crossbelts [34].

2 May 1834 - In order that **sabers** [*sabli*] may be better handled, it is ordered that their hilts [*yefesy*] be reworked according to a new pattern, so that the straight arch [*pryamaya duzhka*], where it joins the headpiece [*golovka*], is sawn off even with the curving part [*sognutaya chast*], while the small flat part [*planochka*] on the grip's brass trim [*mednaya nakladka na grife*], and this trim itself where it is pressed on by the thumb, are to be cut smooth [35].

20 June 1834 - The Nizhnii-Novgorod Dragoon Regiment is ordered to keep the sheepskin **shapka headdresses** worn by them, but to otherwise have a new uniform (Illus. 241) according to the following description: **jacket** [*kurtka*] - of dark-green cloth, with a red cloth collar with dark-green piping on it, dark-green cloth cuffs with red piping; with 6 brass cartridge holders [*napatroniki*] on each side of the chest. Instead of buttons, this jacket is closed by 18 pairs of small wire hooks. Epaulettes remain scaled, of the previous pattern. **Girdle** [*kushak*] - dark-green middle part, red edges, dark-green piping around the girdle. **Sharavary pants** - of cossack pattern, of dark-green cloth with red stripes [*lampasy*] on the side seams and a pocket on the right side. **Cartridge pouch** [*lyadunka*] - of red Russian leather, there being inside of it a wooden holder [*kolodka*] for 18 cartridges. Instead of a crossbelt, there is a leather strap painted red and fastened to the cartridge pouch by three small iron buckles. **Saber** - with a black wooden handle and a scabbard wrapped with black leather. **Swordbelt** [*portupeya*] - of black leather, with two slings [*pasovye remni*] and a sheath [*gnezdo*] for the bayonet, with brass fittings according to a special pattern. **Pistol holder** [*chushka, dlya vkladyvaniya pistoleta*] - of black leather, with two ear-like flaps [*ushka*], these having a similar black leather belt passed through them, with an iron buckle [36].

30 June 1834 - On Dragoon **muskets** the lower small handles [*antabki*] for the sling, instead of being tightly fixed to an ear-shaped bracket set at the trigger guard, are directed to be made with screws [*vmesto ukreplyavshikhsya na-glukho k ushku, vstavlyaemomu v spuskovuyu skobu, poveleno delat na vintakh*]. Moreover, special brackets [*ushki*] with screws drilled into them are to be made for fixing the attachment to the butt (Illus. 242) [37].

3 December 1834 - It is ordered that there are to be no **pistols** in Dragoon regiments [38].

7 December 1834 - Lines [*snury*] for **shakos**, when the latter are being worn, are not to reach to the waist as previously, but only to the middle of the back (Illus. 243) [39].

4 January 1835 - Gloves [*perchatki*] are to be introduced for use by privates, of bluish-grey cloth and made from worn out riding trousers, and worn only at such times as when cloth mittens are worn in infantry forces; non-commissioned officers keep their deerskin gloves as before [40].

15 January 1835 - Mounted non-commissioned officers of Lancer double-squadrons [*Pikinernye diviziony*] are to have one **pistol** each [41].

20 February 1835 - With pistols being withdrawn from Dragoon regiments, the former **ramrods** [*shompoly*] over the cartridge pouches [*lyadunki*] are also withdrawn. Together with this, a new pattern of **bandolier** [*pantaler*], or shoulder belt [*pogonnaya perevyaz*], is confirmed for Lancers [*Pikinery*], with brass fittings, an iron hook, and a strap for the ramrod [*shompolnyi remen*] [42].

13 April 1835 - Officers in formation are to use a toggle [*kostylok*] to fasten one end of the **shako lines** [*kivernyi snur*] in back of the shako to an eye-loop [*petlya*] fashioned from the decorative cord [*etishketnyi snur*]. At all other times when officers are not in formation and must remove the shako, this line is unfastened from the eye-loop and, keeping it around the neck along with its slide [*gaika*], which is to be at the back at the middle of the neck, the end with the toggle is fastened to the second coat button from the top so that the line passes under the right arm and over the pouch-belt (Illus. 244) [43].

19 July 1835 - Approval is given to the following description of a leather **holder** (*chushka*) in which to place the pistol, and the manner of its use:

The holder is of black polished leather, having two leather loops on the back side, i.e. on that side which faces the body, and above on the same side a looped leather strap; and on the outside, opposite the looped strap, there is a leather toggle for fastening. The holder is put onto the swordbelt on the left side and fitted so that it is on the left hip, with the swordbelt and girdle passing through the loops. A whitened, deerskin, 1/2-inch strap, 4 feet 3 inches long, has at one end an elongated slit 1 3/4 inches long; the opposite end is bent back and sewn closed, making a large loop 24 inches long, on which goes a movable, leather loop made of deerskin. This strap is always around the pistol and fastened in the following manner: the end which has the small slit is passed from the left side through the brass trigger guard; then the other end of the strap is passed through this slit and pulled tight; secondly, this strap is wrapped around the narrow part of the butt behind the trigger guard and, passing the end with the loop and keeping that underneath itself, it is tightened again. After this the remaining part of the strap is wound around the narrow part of the butt from the left-hand side to the right, and the end of the large loop is passed from the right side through the brass trigger guard to the hammer on top. In this way the pistol is fitted into its holder and secured by the leather loop and toggle.

When out protecting the flanks [*vo flankirovke*], or during battle, the end of the strap with the large loop is worn around the neck, and so that this loop does not become undone, it is tightened with an movable deerskin ring; the other end, though, always remains secured to the pistol.

When firing has ceased, the pistol is placed into its holder, while the strap remains around the neck if circumstances are foreseen in which the pistol may again be used [44].

22 November 1835 - In all Dragoon regiments, for greater convenience while riding, **copper kettles** are ordered to be lashed not to the left sides of the valises, but to the right [45].

31 January 1836 - Lower ranks' **greatcoats** are to have 12 buttons instead of eleven: six down the front opening, two on the collar patches, two on the shoulder straps, and one behind on the flaps. Along with this lines [*snurki*] are added to the sheepskin **shapkas** of the Nizhnii-Novgorod Regiment: yellow for lower ranks (Illus. 245 and 246), and silver for officers [46].

27 April 1836 - **Lower pompons** [*repeiki*] are ordered to be backed with black leather [47].

5 May 1836 - New **swordbelts** are introduced in all Dragoon regiments except the Nizhnii-Novgorod, with slings [*pasovye remni*] and a strap to the hook for hanging up the saber; these are not movable, but rather are sewn fast to the waist belt [48].

13 May 1836 - Officers' **saddle girths** [*podprugi*] are to be dark green with red stripes [49].

9 October 1836 - As a place for their pistols, staff-trumpeters, trumpeters, and drummers [*shtab-trubachi, trubachi i barabanshchiki*] are to have **holders** [*chushki*], fitted to the saddle over the saddlecloth: on the left side for trumpeters and on the right for drummers. And for cartridges they are to have **cartridge pouches** [*lyadunki*] with crossbelts, as for the other lower ranks (Illus. 247 and 248) [50].

17 January 1837 - When wearing the **frock coat** without the sash, generals and field and company-grade officers are to wear the **saber** under the frock, attaching the upper ring to the hook next to the first sling [*pas*] and putting the hilt through an oblique pocket, in the same way as the half-saber and sword are worn in the Infantry. But when wearing the frock coat with the sash, the saber is to be over the coat, left free on its slings and not hung onto the hook [51].

14 February 1837 - Staff-trumpeters, trumpeters, and drummers who are prescribed pistols when in mounted formation and, for cartridges, cartridge pouches [*lyadunki*] with belts, are also to wear these **cartridge pouches** when in dismounted formation [52].

11 March 1837 - The former muskets in Lancer double-squadrons are replaced with short **carbines** [*karabiny*] of a new pattern (Illus. 249) [53].

15 July 1837 - The new pattern of officers' **sash** is approved, identical with that described above for Grenadier regiments [54].

17 December 1837 - In order to introduce uniformity in the style of officers' **epaulettes**, confirmation is given to the pattern with an additional, fourth, twist of narrow braid (Illus. 250) [55].

11 January 1838 - Approval is given to the description of the officer's **saddle** which was prescribed for use on 6 March 1834, in agreement in all details with the description presented above for Cuirassier regiments [56].

23 February 1838 - Regulations are confirmed concerning the **pistol holders** [*pistoletnyya chushki*] mandated for the saddle on 9 October 1836:

1.) "The holder is to be fastened over the saddlecloth [*valtrap*] on the left side with two straps, passing the encircling strap [*krugovoi remen*] underneath its cover flap.

2.) "For trumpeters the pistol holders are also to be on the left side, but on the right for drummers, straping them to the saddlecloth in the same manner and related in point 1.

3.) "The pistol holder is no longer to be on the swordbelt, while for parades or when on campaign, pistols are to be kept in holders straped to the saddlecloths. On all cavalry exercises and maneuvers the pistol is to be kept on a small strap sewn to the inside of the swordbelt.

4.) "The pistol is to always have its deerskin pistol strap, as prescribed on 19 July 1835. But during all cavalry exercises and maneuvers, in agreement with the preceding point, it is to be worn on the neck as a measure to be taken beforehand, so that those units which will be called upon for flank duty will be in fully and always ready for action." [57].

12 March 1838 - A new pattern of **bandolier belt** [*pantalernyi remen*] is confirmed for Lancer double-squadrons, longer than the cartridge-pouch crossbelt [*lyadunochnaya perevyaz*] and in complete agreement with the description presented above for Cuirassier regiments for 27 November 1828 [58].

17 April 1838 - In His imperial Highness the Heir and Tsesarevich's (the former Moscow) and His imperial Highness the Grand Duke Michael Pavolovich's Regiment (the former Tver), it is ordered that officers' coats have embroidered **gold lace-bars** [*shityya, zolotyya petlitsy*]: one on each side of the collar and three on each cuff flap (Illus. 251) [59].

4 January 1839 - The **riding-trousers** [*reituzy*] of generals and field and company-grade officers are not to have any bows or bands in front [*speredi bantov ne imet*] but rather worn completely plain [*gladkii*] in the manner prescribed for lower ranks [60].

16 October 1840 - The regulation concerning lower ranks' **chevrons** [*shevrony*] is confirmed as laid out above for Grenadier regiments [61].

23 January 1841 - The capes [*bolshie vorotniki*] of officers' **greatcoats** are to be 28 inches long as measured from the bottom edge of the collar [62].

In November of this same year all combatant ranks [*stroevye chiny*] are given a new pattern of **saber** [*sablya*], with a bayonet sheath [*shtykovye nozhny*] for lower ranks (Illus. 252).

26 November 1842 - Until a pattern headdress is confirmed in place of the sheepskin shapka, officers and combatant lower ranks of the Nizhnii-Novgorod Dragoon Regiment are directed to wear **forage caps** [63].

31 January 1843 - The **lances** [*piki*] in the regiments are to be reworked according to the new pattern, so that the shaft [*drevko*] with its endpiece [*nakonechnik*] measures 10 1/2 feet [64].

8 April 1843 - The bands on **forage caps** in all Dragoon regiments are ordered to be dark green with two pipings in the regimental color [65].

8 April 1843 - Officers and combatant lower ranks (except in the Nizhnii-Novgorod Regiment) are given new **shakos**, the same size as those received at this same time by regiments of Army Infantry and described above for Grenadier regiments (Illus. 253) [66].

Along with this, in order to distinguish rank among the lower ranks, lace [*nashivki*] is to be sewn onto **epaulettes** according to the following directions:

1.) For senior sergeants [*starshie vakhtmistry*] — wide gold galloon, sewn in one row across the shoulder straps (Illus. 254a).

2.) For distinguished officer candidates [*portupei-yunkera*] and officer candidates [*yunkera*] — narrow gold galloon along the edges of the epaulettes (Illus. 254b).

3.) For junior sergeants [*mladshchie vakhtmistry*] — narrow white woollen tape [*bason*], sewn on in three rows across the shoulder strap (Illus. 255a).

4.) For non-commissioned officers [*unter-ofitsery*] — the same tape sewn on in the same way, in two rows (Illus. 255b).

5.) For lance-corporals [*yefreitory*] — the same lace sewn on in the same way, in one row (Illus. 256).

The same galloon and tape is prescribed for the shoulder straps of greatcoats, following the scheme described above for Grenadier and Cuirassier regiments [67].

10 May 1843 - Cover flaps [*kryshki*] for **cartridge pouches** [*lyadunki*] are to be (with the cover sewn to the box): 8 inches long, 9 inches wide at the top edge, and 10 inches wide along the bottom edge. The oval **belt rings** for carbines are to be replaced with circular ones. Belts are attached to the stocks [*lozhi*] of the carbines by means of special straps with buckles, and in order to avoid the upper brass band hitting the spurs, as well as so that the carbines do not drag on the ground when dismounted, they are to be raised up by shortening the bandolier, according to the height of the individual [68].

2 June 1843 - Approval is given to the same manner of affixing the **shako plate** and badges for distinction as is presented above for Grenadier regiments [69].

2 January 1844 - Officers are to have a **cockade** on the band of the forage cap, as related above for Grenadier regiments [70].

19 February 1844 - The shortening of the **bandolier** as established on 10 May 1843, in accordance with an individual's height, is to be done by means of a brass buckle on its end, so that below it is even with the lower edge of the coat [71].

9 May 1844 - Shakos are replaced by **helmets** [*kaski*] with plumes [*sultany*], of the same pattern and in accordance with the same regulations as for Grenadier regiments, but with the addition of a metal edging [*obodok*] on the front peak, of the same color as the helmet mountings (Illus. 257) [72].

1844 May 20 - A new scheme for the various **forage caps** of lower ranks is confirmed, based on which they remain dark green as before, while the piping around the top is to be: in the 1st double-squadron [*divizion*] — red, in the 2nd — white, in the 3rd — light blue, in the 4th - blue, in the 5th - yellow, and in the replacement [*zapasnyi*] and reserve [*rezervnyi*] squadrons — dark green. The cap band is prescribed to be the same color as the coat's facing cloth, with two dark-green pipings around both edges, and with the cut-out number of the squadron and the Cyrillic letter E [for *eskadron* — M.C.]. When the cap band is yellow, the numeral and letter are to be on red cloth, and for other colors they are to be on yellow. For officers of all double-squadrons the cap band is the same as the lower ranks', with two dark-green pipings, but without a numeral or letter, while the piping around the top of the forage cap is the same color as the band [73].

21 September 1844 - **Non-commissioned officer standard-bearers** [*shtandartnye unter-ofitsery*] in formation are to always have the cartridge pouch under the crossbelt for the standard [74].

4 January 1845 - Officers' **helmets** are to have, on the right side under the chin-scales, a cockade, as described above for Grenadier regiments (Illus. 258) [75].

15 November 1845 - All regiments are to have **pioneer axes** [*shantsovye topory*], two for each platoon [*vzvod*]. Additionally, there are to be 56 iron **spades** [*lopaty*] in each regiment, as referred to for Cuirassier regiments [76].

19 November 1845 - On the **lances**, the clamps [*skoby*] which come out of the sharp upper end and blunt lower end to hold them to the shaft, as well as the small "ears" in which the lance sling [*temlyak*] goes, are to be painted the same color as the shafts, as was done on the lances of the previous pattern [77].

13 September 1846 - Officers' **pistols** are to be of the new pattern with a percussion lock [*udarnye zamki*], for which new carriers [*kobury*] are approved, made to fit their locks, as related in detail above for Army Cuirassier regiments [78].

19 May 1847 - With the new general directive concerning the colors for **forage caps** within the War Department [*Voennoe vedomstvo*, i.e. the entire army — M.C.], the clerks, medics [*feldshera*], and other lower ranks of Army Dragoon regiments with dark-green forage caps are to have cap bands and piping around the top part in the same colors as the cap bands and piping of combatant lower ranks. However, barbers [*tsiryulniki*], hospital orderlies [*lazaretnye sluzhiteli*], and others with grey forage caps are to have piping on both edges of the cap band and around the top in the same color as the regiment's facing cloth [79].

7 July 1847 - **Regimental adjutants** [*Polkovye adyutanty*] in mounted formation are to have horses of the color prescribed for the regiments, not forbidding whomever wishes, however, to also have grey horses [80].

31 August 1847 - Under all circumstances in which lower ranks of Dragoon regiments now wear their **greatcoats** thrown back [*v-nakidku*], they are directed to wear them using the sleeves, over any personal equipment, and open [*v-raspashku*] (Illus. 259) [81].

5 November 1847 - **Greatcoats** worn using the sleeves, open and over personal equipment, are to be worn only in mounted order (Illus. 259). However, the wearing of greatcoats in dismounted order is left according to the previous manner [82].

17 November 1847 - All Dragoon regiments are ordered to have leather cases [*kozhanye chekhly*] for their **muskets**, with straps and buckles, following the example of the Dragoon and Horse-Grenadier regiments of the Life-Guards (Illus. 260 and 261) [83].

9 January 1848 - Field and company-grade officers of Dragoon regiments, on those days when after guard mount [*posle* *razvoda*] they must remain in holiday uniform [*prazdnichnaya forma*], are allowed to wear, for walking out [*dlya progulok*], their prescribed **frock coats** and **riding trousers** along with **helmets** with plumes [84].

19 January 1848 - With the introduction of officers' pistols with percussion locks, Highest Authority confirms the description of the **firing-cap pouch** [*kapsyulnaya sumochka*] worn with the cartridge pouch that is described in detail above for Army Cuirassier regiments [85].

24 January 1848 - Deerskin **swordbelts** [*losinnyya portupei*] are to be introduced for the regiments of the 1st and 2nd Dragoon Divisions, following the pattern used in His Royal Highness the Crown Prince of Württemberg's Dragoon Regiment (formerly the Nizhnii-Novgorod), wearing them over the shoulder and over the coat and frock coat (Illus. 262) [86].

20 February 1848 - For officers these **swordbelts** are to be of gold galloon on black leather, based on the color of the buttons [87].

25 April 1848 - The **valise's flap** [*klapan na chemodane*] with buttons is completely done away with [88].

24 December 1849 - The grips of the **gold swords** awarded for bravery are to be gold instead of wrapped with black lacquered leather [89].

5 March 1850 - **Bandoliers** for standards are ordered to be 4 3/8 inches wide, 4 1/2 feet long, and lined with cloth as follows:

For HIS IMPERIAL HIGHNESS THE HEIR AND TSESAREVICH'S Regiment: - red on the outside, dark green on the inside; fringes, galloon, and the hook with bracket are gold.

For HIS IMPERIAL HIGHNESS THE GRAND DUKE CONSTANTINE NIKOLAEVICH'S Regiment: - white on the outside, dark green on the inside; fringes, galloon, and the hook with bracket are gold.

For the Kinburn Regiment: - yellow on the outside, dark green on the inside; fringes, galloon, and the hook with bracket are gold.

For the New Russia Regiment: - light blue on the outside, dark green on the inside; fringes, galloon, and the hook with bracket are gold.

For His Highness Prince Emil of Hesse's Regiment: - red on the outside, dark green on the inside; fringes, galloon, and the hook with bracket are gold.

For the Riga Regiment: - white on the outside, dark green on the inside; fringes, galloon, and the hook with bracket are gold.

For the Finland Regiment: - yellow on the outside, dark green on the inside; fringes, galloon, and the hook with bracket are gold.

For HIS IMPERIAL HIGHNESS THE GRAND DUKE NICHOLAS NIKOLAEVICH'S Regiment: - light blue on the outside, dark green on the inside; fringes, galloon, and the hook with bracket are gold.

For His Royal Highness the Crown Prince of Württemberg's Regiment: - red on the outside, dark green on the inside; fringes, galloon, and the hook with bracket are gold [90].

30 March 1851 - With the introduction of smaller **bandoliers** [*pantalery*] and crossbelts with a movable **firing-cap pouch** [*perevyazi s peredvizhnoyu kapsyulnoyu sumochkoyu*] fitted onto a small iron hook, approval is given to the description of them that is presented in detail above for Army Cuirassier regiments (Illus. 265) [91].

15 April 1851 - Approval is given to the description for fitting straps to the **valise** for dismounted lower ranks and prescribed to also be in effect for personnel released on leave from Cavalry units, as laid out in detail above for Cuirassier regiments [92].

3 January 1852 - The cases or coverings [*chekhly, ili nakladki*] introduced for Army Infantry on 8 July 1851 for the **firing nipples** [*sterzhni*] of percussion weapons are ordered to be used on percussion firearms in Cavalry forces (Illus. 266) [93].

16 July 1852 - Cases or coverings for the **firing nipples** of percussion weapons of Army Cavalry forces are to be according to the description confirmed by Highest Authority on 8 July 1851, and laid out in detail above for Cuirassier regiments (Illus. 266) [94].

29 September 1852 - With the appointment of **HIS IMPERIAL HIGHNESS THE GRAND DUKE MICHAEL NIKOLAEVICH** as honorary colonel [*Shef*] of the Kinburn Cuirassier Regiment, field and company-grade officers of this regiment are to have gold lace bars on the collar and cuffs-flaps of the coat [*kolet* - sic, a mistake by Viskovatov? *Kolet* should refer to the style of coat worn by cuirassiers, while dragoons would wear the more usual *mundir* - M.C.] (Illus. 267) [95].

18 February 1854 - The regulation of 15 November 1853 concerning light-cavalry **horse furniture**, presented above in the section for Army Cuirassier regiments, is also extended to Dragoon regiments (Illus. 268) [96].

29 April 1854 - During wartime, generals and field and company-grade officers are to have **campaign greatcoats** [*pokhodnyya shineli*] of the same color and pattern as the greatcoats of lower ranks, based on the rules explained above for Grenadier regiments (Illus. 268) [97].

10 October 1854 - His Royal Highness the Crown Prince of Württemberg's Dragoon Regiment is granted gold **lace-bars** for the collars and cuffs of officers' jackets [*kurtki*] (Illus. 269) [98].

NOTES TO THE ILLUSTRATIONS
By Mark Conrad

213. Since 1807, dragoons wore dark green like the infantry. By an order of 1817, facings and metal appointments were as follows: Moscow — rose/silver. Kargopol — red/silver. Kinburn — yellow/silver. New Russia — sky blue/silver. Kazan — raspberry/gold. Riga — red/gold. Tver — light blue/gold. Finland — white/gold. St.-Petersburg — rose/gold. Kharkov — orange/gold. Smolensk — yellow/gold. Courland — sky blue/gold. Ingermanland — light blue/silver. Narva — orange/silver. Kiev — raspberry/silver. Mitau — white/silver Nizhnii-Novgorod — brick/silver.

The shako cords were white (silver for officers, and mixed white/orange/black for non-commissioned officers). Shako plates were the same color as the buttons. Pompons were red for privates and trumpeters, of the hourglass pattern for non-commissioned officers and staff-trumpeters, and silver for officers. Epaulettes for lower ranks were white or yellow worsted, depending on the buttons. Black leather reinforcement on the trousers. The black leather cartridge pouch had a round badge with an eagle, in the button color. Officers' pouches were silver with a gold eagle. Lower ranks' waistbelts and crossbelts were white; officers' pouch belts were gold or silver, but the plate, prickers, and chains were always silver. Sabers had brass hilts and steel scabbards. White sword slings.

In 1817, the swallows' nests for drummers and trumpeters were ordered to be in the facing color, with 1/2 inch wide white tape. Dark-green saddlecloth with a broad stripe and piping in the facing color, separated by dark green. The monogram on the saddlecloth is also in the facing color for lower ranks, but in silver or gold for officers. At the rear of the saddle, there is a white sack for forage in front of the grey valise.

214. Dark-green forage cap with band and piping in the facing color.

217. The cuffs on the frock coat were in the facing color.

218. The plume consists of white feathers over orange and black.

219. The collar and shoulder straps of the greatcoat were in the facing color.

220. For the non-commissioned officer, a thin strip of facing color can be seen on the edge of the cuffs and collar, outside the lace that marks his rank.

224. The short strip of lace depicted above the epaulette is the cross-strap holding the epaulette to the shoulder of the coat. Only the edges of the cross-strap are in the facing color, since the rest is covered by the gold or silver lace.

225. The Viskovatov illustrators vary in their depictions of the piping around the cuff flaps of Dragoons. It is also difficult to be sure what is in fact depicted due to what would be the near invisibility of dark-green piping on a dark-green background.

225 and 226. The lack of piping on the bottom edge of the cuff flap is an artist's error in Viskovatov. The greatcoat collar is in the facing color, piped dark-green.

228. Contrary to the text, there is no piping on the collar.

234. For the regiments on the left, the two rectangles are white and the stripe and tails are in the facing color. For the regiments on the right, it is the tails and stripe which are white.

235. The girdle is in the facing color, with a dark-green middle stripe and piping on the outside.

237. The Viskovatov artist shows the officer's pants piping as a little too wide. This plate is reproduced in color in Alla Begunov's 1992 book *Sabli, ostryi, koni bystry...*, which shows the lance shaft as the same bright blue as the facings. The officer's pouch belt is gold, with silver fittings, and the pouch itself is silver with a gold eagle. The turnbacks are dark green with blue edges.

241. For the officer, the black cartridge holders have metal tops, and are horizontally striped with two rows of lace, with the first row of lace being at the bottom. Officers also have lace around the bottom and sides of each set of cartridge holders. The private's cartridge holders are dark with metal tops.

245. The black cartridge pouch appears to have a light colored edging.

248. The drum is carried on a white belt and has white tensioners. The hoops have white and black triangles, with the white ones pointing out on both top and bottom.

253. The illustrator has misspelled the second Cyrillic "i" in "otlichie".

258. Contrary to the text, there is apparently no piping on the cuffs or cuff-flaps.

259 and 260. The greatcoat collars are dark green with piping and tabs in the facing colors.

261. All black case.

263. The collar is as on the full-dress coat; cuffs are dark green piped in the facing color.

265. This plate is also reproduced in color by Begunov. The lance shaft appears to be the same red as the color on the pennon. The lance sling is reddish brown leather. The crossbelts, swordbelt, and straps for the ramrod are all white. The small pouch on the front of the crossbelt is black. The reins and other horse harness are black, including the knobs on the chest strap and forehead strap.

8. HORSE-JÄGER REGIMENTS *(KONNO-YEGERSKIE POLKI)*.

11 February 1826 - Clerks [*pisarya*] and in general all non-combatant lower ranks are ordered to have grey **riding trousers** [*reituzy*] with stripes [*lampasy*] [99].

10 June 1826 - Instead of the dark-green pants [*pantalony*] with stripes, it is ordered that grey cloth **riding trousers** without stripes always be worn, with piping on the side seam according to the color of the collar (Illus. 270, 271, 272, and 273) [100].

15 September 1826 - Lower ranks who have served out the regulation number of years without reproach and who voluntarily remain on service are ordered to wear **gold galloon** [*nashivka iz zolotago galuna*] sewn onto the left sleeve, as related above for Cuirassier regiments [101].

1 January 1827 - In order to distinguish **rank**, it is ordered that officers' epaulettes are to have small forged and stamped stars [*kovannyya zvezdochki*] of the same appearance and according to the same scheme as related above for Grenadier regiments [102].

31 July 1827 - Numbers and letters on **shako covers** [*kivernye chekhly*] are directed to be in yellow oil paints [103].

13 October 1827 - All combatant ranks are given scaled **epaulettes** [*cheshuichatye epolety*] the same color as the buttons, based on those described above for Dragoon regiments (Illus. 274) [104].

14 December 1827 - The **lace** [*nashivka*] sewn onto lower ranks' left sleeves, instituted on 15 September 1826, is to be silver, of non-commissioned officers' galloon [105].

9 February 1828 - The previous **shakos** [*kivera*] in Horse-Jäger regiments are replaced with new ones of the same pattern as established at this same time for Dragoon regiments but with white appointments, pompons, and cords (Illus. 275) [106].

7 March 1828 - Lower ranks who return to their regiments from the Model Cavalry Regiment, as well as those who have previously been in the Instructional Cavalry Squadron, are to have yellow **tape** [*bason*] sewn onto the shoulder straps of the greatcoat, of the same pattern as described in detail above for Grenadier regiments. The same tape is also ordered to be on epaulettes [107].

24 April 1828 - Instead of the grey coats [*mundiry serago sveta*] previously used by them, all **noncombatant** non-commissioned officers are given dark-green frock coats with one row of buttons [*temnozelenye, odnobortnye syurtuki*] and the same collar, cuffs, and shoulder straps as for combatants, while the pants [*pantalony*] are grey with piping on the side seams in the same color as the collar. Instead of their previous coats [*mundiry*], non-combatant master-craftsmen lower ranks [*masterovye nestroevye nizhnie chiny*], as well as infirmary orderlies [*lazaretynye sluzhiteli*], are to wear jackets of grey cloth, with distinctions as on the coats [*kurtki serago sukna, po obraztsu mundirov*], while pants are as for the preceding non-combatants [108].

20 December 1828 - A new pattern for the **shako plate** is confirmed based on those established on 24 April 1828 for Infantry and Jäger regiments, but made from white tin (silver for officers), as well as with a cut-out figure of the regiment's assigned number (Illus. 276): in the Severskii Regiment - 1, Chernigov - 2, Nezhin - 3, Dorpat - 4, Pereyaslavl - 5, His Highness the King of Württemberg's - 6, Arzamas - 7, and Tiraspol - 8. In the King of Württemberg's Regiment, there are also badges with the cut-out inscription: "*Za otlichie*" ["For excellence"], following the model of similar badges in the Infantry [109].

16 December 1829 - The cuffs of officers' **frock coats** [*syurtuki*] are to be the same color as the frock instead of being colored, with piping of the same color as the collar patch on the coat [*mundir*] [110].

26 December 1829 - All combatant ranks are ordered to have uniform **buttons** with the raised image of the numeral prescribed for the shako plate [111].

24 September 1830 - The lining [*podkladka*] of officers' **frock coats** is ordered to be dark green like the color of the frock coat itself [112].

1 January 1832 - Generals who have **gold swords**, decorated with diamonds and with the inscription "*Za khrabost*" ["For courage"], are to wear these without swordknots [113].

3 January 1833 - **Covers** for shakos are discontinued [114].

20 January 1833 - **Covers** for shakos are kept as before [115].

22 February 1833 - Field and company-grade officers are not to wear hats, but at all times be in **shakos** [116].

16 March 1833 - **Undress coats** [*vitse-mundiry*] for field and company-grade officers are abolished, with only generals being allowed to wear them [117].

21 March 1833 - A HIGHEST Order is issued for reorganizing the Cavalry and with it Horse-Jäger regiments are **disbanded** [118].

270. White metal buttons and shako fittings; by regulation, a green pompon on the front of the shako (although in Viskovatov's plates it appears white); white shako cords, dark-green coats, dark-green collars with patches and piping in the facing color; cuffs, piping, and edging on the dark-green turnbacks all in the facing color; piping on the pants in the facing color; shoulder straps in the facing color; white gloves; crown, monogram, stripe, and piping on the dark-green saddle cloth in the facing color; white crossbelt and waistbelt with brass fittings; the cartridge pouch was black leather with a round tin plate bearing the image of a double-headed eagle; steel scabbard and sword hilt; white sword slings; dark-green forage cap with piping and band in the facing color. At the rear of the saddle, there is a white sack for forage in front of the grey valise. At this time, the riding trousers for all the cavalry were changing from blue-grey to plain grey, but this is not mentioned in the text.

Since 1816, the facing colors for the regiments were as follows: Severskii - orange, Chernigov - white, Nezhin - turquoise, Dorpat - rose, Pereyaslavl - raspberry, King of Württemburg's (previously the Livonia) - red, Arzamas - light blue, Tiraspol - yellow.

By an order of 1823, horses in each regiment were to be: Severskii - chestnut, Chernigov - black, Nezhin - grey, Dorpat - bay, Pereyaslavl - chestnut, King of Württemburg's - black, Arzamas - grey, Tiraspol - bay.

According to Zweguintzow, lances were issued for the campaign in Poland and then withdrawn by an order of 12 August 1831, it being unknown whether or not they had pennons.

271. Pants reinforced with leather. The grey greatcoat has a collar and shoulder straps as on the dress coat, except that the collar's base color was grey. Silver non-commissioned officers' galloon. Zweguintzow notes that Viskovatov's plates show that around 1826 or 1827 the bands of forage caps changed to dark-green with two rows of piping in the facing color, but this is not mentioned in the text.

272. Trumpeters had white musicians' tape on their coats. Staff-trumpeters additionally had non-commissioned officers' galloon on the top and front of the collar and around the cuffs. The swallow's nests on the shoulders had white tape over the facing color.

273. Officers had silver metal appointments. Epaulettes, pouchbelts and fittings, and pouches were all silver. The lining of the epaulette and the small cross straps was in the facing color. The crown and monogram on the saddlecloth was in silver.

274. The officer's undress coat [*vitse-mundir*] was dark green with long tails, without tail pockets, and with the collar, cuffs, and lining as on the dress coat. This plate shows the turnbacks to be dark green piped in the facing color. The plume on the black hat had white feathers over black and orange.

276. The private of the Tiraspol Regiment has a badge for distinction on his shako, but this must be an error since only the King of Württemburg's Regiment was so entitled.

9. LANCER REGIMENTS *(ULANSKIE POLKI).*

11 February 1826 - Clerks [*pisarya*] and in general all lower ranks are ordered to have grey **riding trousers** [*reituzy*] with stripes [*lampasy*] [119].

10 June 1826 - For all Lancer regiments except those in the 1st and Lithuania Lancer Divisions (Vladimir, Siberia, Orenburg, Yamburg, Polish, Tatar, Lithuania, and Volhynia regiments), instead of the dark-blue pants [*sinie pantalony*] with stripes and grey campaign riding trousers [*pokhodnye reituzy*], also with stripes, it is ordered that grey cloth **riding trousers** without stripes always be worn, with piping on the side seam according to the color of the collar. At the same time, all Lancer regiments are given round **pompons** for the headdress [*shapka*]: of white wool for lower ranks and in silver for officers (Illus. 277, 278, 279, 280, 281, 282, 283, and 284) [120].

15 September 1826 - Lower ranks who have served out the regulation number of years without reproach and who voluntarily remain on service are ordered to wear **gold galloon** [*nashivka iz zolotago galuna*] sewn onto the left sleeve, as related above for Cuirassier regiments [121].

1 January 1827 - In order to distinguish rank, it is ordered that officers' **epaulettes** are to have small forged and stamped stars of the same appearance and according to the same scheme as for the preceding Cavalry regiments [122].

26 February 1827 - Lower ranks in the regiments of the 1st Lancer Division are ordered to have the grey **riding trousers** established on 10 June 1826 (Illus. 285 and 286). Thereafter dark-blue pants with stripes are retained only for officers of this division [123].

15 May 1827 - Officers' coats in **HIS IMPERIAL HIGHNESS THE GRAND DUKE MICHAEL PAVLOVICH'S Lancer Regiment** (formerly the Vladimir Regiment) are directed to have lace-bars [*petlitsy*] in the style of the L.-Gds. Lancer Regiment, but in silver (Illus. 287) [124].

31 July 1827 - Numbers and letters on **headdress covers** [*chekhly shapok*] are directed to be in yellow oil paints [125].

6 October 1827 - These former Dragoon regiments, renamed and forming the **4th Lancer Division**: St.-Petersburg, Kharkov, Smolensk, and Courland, are assigned the following uniform colors:

St.-Petersburg Regiment	collar, cuffs, plastron [*latskany*], piping, stripes on the girdle [*kushak*], headdress, edge of the saddle cloth, and lower half of the pennon - all orange (Illus. 288).
Kharkov Regiment	collar, cuffs, plastron, piping, stripes on the girdle, headdress, edge of the saddle cloth, and lower half of the pennon - all blue [*sinii*] (Illus. 289).
Smolensk Regiment	collar, cuffs, plastron, piping, stripes on the girdle, headdress, edge of the saddle cloth, and lower half of the pennon - all yellow (Illus. 290).
Courland Regiment	collar, cuffs, plastron, piping, stripes on the girdle, headdress, edge of the saddle cloth, and lower half of the pennon - all light blue [*svetlosinii*] (Illus. 290).

In all four regiments, the jackets [*kurtki*], collar patches, saddle cloths, and girdles are dark blue [*temnosinii*]; buttons, epaulettes, and the upper half of the pennon are white [126].

13 October 1827 - All combatant ranks are given **scaled epaulettes** [*cheshuichatye epolety*] the same color as their buttons and with a cloth backing the same color as the combatant headdresses, on the same basis as related above for Dragoon regiments [127].

14 December 1827 - The **lace** [*nashivka*] sewn onto lower ranks' left sleeves, instituted on 15 September 1826, is to be silver, of non-commissioned officers' galloon.

In this same year the regiments of the Lithuania Lancer Division were permitted to have black sheep's fleece **saddlecloths** instead of cloth ones (Illus. 291) [128].

26 January 1828 - For officers' headdresses, the small chain [*tsepochka*] on the **chinstrap** [*podborodnyi remen*] is replaced by standard shako chinstrap scales (Illus. 291) [129].

7 March 1828 - Lower ranks who return to their regiments from the Model Cavalry Regiment, as well as those who have previously been in the Instructional Cavalry Squadron, are to have yellow tape [*bason*] sewn onto the **shoulder straps** of the greatcoat, of the same appearance as for Dragoon regiments. The same tape is also ordered to be on epaulettes [130].

24 March 1828 - The uniform **coats** of lower ranks are forbidden to have cinches [*peretyazhki*] [131].

20 December 1828 - A new pattern for the **headdress plate** is confirmed based on those established on 24 April 1828 for Infantry and Jäger regiments, but of white tin (silver for officers), and likewise with a cut-out figure of the regiment's assigned number (Illus. 292): in HIS IMPERIAL HIGHNESS THE GRAND DUKE MICHAEL PAVLOVICH'S Lancers - 1, Siberia - 2, Orenburg - 3, Yamburg - 4, Belgorod - 5, Chuguev - 6, Borisoglebsk - 7, Serpukhov - 8, 1st Ukraine - 9, 2nd Ukraine - 10, 3rd Ukraine - 11, 4th Ukraine - 12, St. Petersburg - 13, Kharkov - 14, Smolensk - 15, Courland - 16, 1st Bug - 17, 2nd Bug - 18, 3rd Bug - 19, 4th Bug - 20, Polish - 21, Tatar - 22, Lithuania - 23, and Volhynia - 24 [132].

17 November 1829 - With the renaming of the 4th Lancer Division as the 5th, and of the Bug Lancer Division as the 4th, the regiments in these divisions are assigned new **numbers** as follows: 1st Bug - 13, 2nd - 14, 3rd - 15, 4th - 16, St. Petersburg - 17, Kharkov - 18, Smolensk - 19, and Courland - 20 [133].

16 December 1829 - Instead of being colored, the cuffs of officers' **frock coats** [*syurtuki*] are to be the same color as the frock, with piping of the same color as the piping on the jacket [*kurtka*] (Illus. 293) [134].

26 December 1829 - All combatant ranks are ordered to have uniform **buttons** with the raised image of the numeral prescribed for the shako plate [sic, should be *headdress* plate - M.C.] [135].

6 April 1830 - The Courland, Smolensk, and Kharkov Lancer Regiments are awarded **badges** for their headdresses [*znaki na shapki*] with the inscription: "*Za otlichie*" ["For excellence"], following the model of these same badges in the Army Infantry [136].

25 July 1830 - With the renaming of the 1st Bug Lancer Regiment as the *Voznesensk*, the 2nd Bug as the *Olviopol*, the 3rd Bug as the *Bug*, and the 4th Bug as the *Odessa*, the **uniform** of the former 1st Bug Regiment is assigned to the Bug Regiment, that of the 2nd - to the Odessa (Illus. 294), that of the 3rd - to the Voznesensk, and that of the 4th - to the Olviopol (Illus. 295) [137].

24 September 1830 - The lining [*podkladka*] of officers' **frock coats** is to be dark blue [*sinii*] like the color of the frock coat itself [138].

25 November 1830 - In the regiments of the Lithuania Lancer Division dark-blue **pants with stripes** are kept only for officers (Illus. 296 and 297) [139].

6 December 1831 - The Ukraine Lancer Regiment (formerly the 1st Ukraine), the Novo-Arkhangelsk (formerly the 2nd Ukraine), the Novo-Mirgorod (formerly the 3rd Ukraine), and the Yelisavetgrad (formerly the 4th Ukraine) are granted **headdress badges** inscribed: "*Za otlichie*" [140].

26 December 1831 - In the regiments of the 1st and 6th (formerly the Lithuania) Lancer Divisions, the dark-blue **pants with stripes** which were kept for officers are withdrawn [141].

30 December 1831 - In the **Polish Lancer Regiment**, the headdresses, facing cloth on the uniforms and saddlecloths, and the lower half of the pennons, are ordered to be orange instead of raspberry (Illus. 298).

In this same year the fleece **saddlecloths** of the regiments in the 6th Lancer Division were withdrawn [142].

3 January 1833 - **Covers for headdresses** are discontinued [143].

20 January 1833 - These **covers** are kept as before [144].

21 March 1833 - With the general reorganization of the Army Cavalry and the disbandment of the Polish and Tatar Lancer Regiments, the other Lancer regiments are directed to adopt **uniforms** as follows:

Belgorod - That of His imperial highness the Grand Duke Michael Pavlovich's Regiment, but without lace-bars.

Chuguev - That of the Siberia Regiment.

Borisoglebsk - That of the Orenburg Regiment.

Serpukhov - That of the Yamburg Regiment.

Ukraine - That of the Belgorod Regiment.

Novo-Arkhangelsk - That of the Chuguev Regiment.

Novo-Mirgorod - That of the Borisoglebsk Regiment.

Yelisavetgrad - That of the Serpukhov Regiment.

St. Petersburg - That of the Smolensk Regiment.

Smolensk - That of the St. Petersburg Regiment.

Siberia - That of the Tatar Regiment.

Orenburg - That of the Polish Regiment.

His imperial highness the Grand Duke Michael Pavlovich's - That of the Novo-Mirgorod, but with silver lace-bars.

Yamburg - That of the Yelisavetgrad Regiment.

Consequently the colors for the uniform, saddlecloth, and pennon; the numbers on headdress plates and buttons; and the colors for horses are as follows:

St.-Petersburg Regiment	yellow collar, plastron, cuffs, piping, stripes on the girdle, headdress, backing to the epaulettes, edge of the saddlecloth, and lower half of the pennon; dark-blue [*sinii*] collar patches; number 1; sorrel [*ryzhie*] horses (Illus. 299).
Courland Regiment	light-blue [*svetlosinii*] collar, plastron, cuffs, piping, stripes on the girdle, headdress, backing to the epaulettes, edge of the saddlecloth, and lower half of the pennon; dark-blue collar patches; number 2; black [*voronye*] horses, with bays [*karie*] and dark chestnuts [*temnognedye*] allowed to be included (Illus. 300).
Smolensk Regiment	orange collar, plastron, cuffs, piping, stripes on the girdle, headdress, backing to the epaulettes, edge of the saddlecloth, and lower half of the pennon; dark-blue collar patches; number 3; chestnut [*gnedye*] horses (Illus. 301).
Kharkov Regiment	white collar, plastron, cuffs, piping, stripes on the girdle, headdress, backing to the epaulettes, and edge of the saddlecloth; dark-blue lower half of the pennon and collar patches; number 4; grey [*serye*] horses (Illus. 301).
Lithuania Regiment	dark-blue [*sinii*] collar; yellow collar patches, plastron, cuffs, piping, stripes on the girdle, headdress, backing to the epaulettes, edge of the saddlecloth, and lower half of the pennon; number 5; sorrel horses (Illus. 302).
Volhynia Regiment	dark-blue collar; light-blue [*svetlosinii*] collar patches, plastron, cuffs, piping, stripes on the girdle, headdress, backing to the epaulettes, edge of the saddlecloth, and lower half of the pennon; number 6; black horses, with bays and dark chestnuts allowed to be included (Illus. 302).
Orenburg Regiment	dark-blue collar; orange collar patches, plastron, cuffs, piping, stripes on the girdle, headdress, backing to the epaulettes, edge of the saddlecloth, and lower half of the pennon; number 7; chestnut horses (Illus. 303).
Siberia Regiment	dark-blue collar; white collar patches, plastron, cuffs, piping, stripes on the girdle, headdress, backing to the epaulettes, and edge of the saddlecloth; dark-blue lower half of the pennon; number 8; grey horses (Illus. 303).

Voznesensk Regiment	dark-blue collar without patches; yellow plastron, cuffs, piping, stripes on the girdle, headdress, backing to the epaulettes, edge of the saddlecloth, and lower half of the pennon; dark-blue piping on the riding trousers; number 9; sorrel horses (Illus. 304).
Olviopol Regiment	dark-blue collar without patches; light-blue plastron, cuffs, piping, stripes on the girdle, headdress, backing to the epaulettes, edge of the saddlecloth, and lower half of the pennon; dark-blue piping on the riding trousers; number 10; black horses, with bays and dark chestnuts allowed to be included (Illus. 304).
Bug Regiment	dark-blue collar without patches; orange plastron, cuffs, piping, stripes on the girdle, headdress, backing to the epaulettes, edge of the saddlecloth, and lower half of the pennon; dark-blue piping on the riding trousers; number 11; grey horses (Illus. 305).
Odessa Regiment	dark-blue collar without patches; white plastron, cuffs, piping, stripes on the girdle, headdress, backing to the epaulettes, and edge of the saddlecloth; dark-blue lower half of the pennon and piping on the riding trousers; number 12; chestnut horses (Illus. 305).
HIH the Grand Duke Michael Pavlovich's *Lancers*	yellow collar, plastron, cuffs, piping, stripes on the girdle, headdress, backing to the epaulettes, edge of the saddlecloth, and lower half of the pennon; number 13; sorrel horses (Illus. 306).
Yamburg Regiment	light-blue collar, plastron, cuffs, piping, stripes on the girdle, headdress, backing to the epaulettes, edge of the saddlecloth, and lower half of the pennon; number 14; black horses, with bays and dark chestnuts allowed to be included (Illus. 306).
Belgorod Regiment	red collar, plastron, cuffs, piping, stripes on the girdle, headdress, backing to the epaulettes, edge of the saddlecloth, and lower half of the pennon; number 15; chestnut horses (Illus. 307).
Chuguev Regiment	red collar, plastron, cuffs, piping, stripes on the girdle, and edge of the saddlecloth; white headdress and backing to the epaulettes; dark-blue lower half of the pennon; number 16; grey horses (Illus. 307).
Borisoglebsk Regiment	red collar, plastron, cuffs, piping, stripes on the girdle, and edge of the saddlecloth; yellow headdress, backing to the epaulettes, and lower half of the pennon; number 17; sorrel horses (Illus. 308).
Serpukhov Regiment	red collar, plastron, cuffs, piping, stripes on the girdle, and edge of the saddlecloth; light-blue headdress, backing to the epaulettes, and lower half of the pennon; number 18; black horses, with bays and dark chestnuts allowed to be included (Illus. 308).
Ukraine Regiment	dark-blue collar without patches; red plastron, cuffs, piping, stripes on the girdle, headdress, backing to the epaulettes, edge of the saddlecloth, and lower half of the pennon; dark-blue piping on the riding trousers; number 19; chestnut horses (Illus. 309).
Novo-Arkhangelsk Regiment	dark-blue collar without patches; red plastron, cuffs, piping, stripes on the girdle, and edge of the saddlecloth; white headdress and backing to the epaulettes; dark blue lower half of the pennon and piping on the riding trousers; number 20; bay horses, but grey in the future (Illus. 309).
Novo-Mirgorod Regiment	dark-blue collar without patches; red plastron, cuffs, piping, stripes on the girdle, and edge of the saddlecloth; yellow headdress, backing to the epaulettes, and lower half of the pennon; dark-blue piping on the riding trousers; number 21; sorrel horses (Illus. 310).
Yelisavetgrad Regiment	dark-blue collar without patches; red plastron, cuffs, piping, stripes on the girdle, and edge of the saddlecloth; light-blue headdress, backing to the epaulettes, and lower half of the pennon; dark-blue piping on the riding trousers; number 22; black horses, with bays and dark chestnuts allowed to be included (Illus. 311).

In all these regiments, buttons and other similarly colored items remain white, as before. It is ordered that the headdresses of the St.-Petersburg, Courland, Smolensk, Kharkov, Ukraine, Novo-Arkhangelsk, and Yelisavetgrad regiments have the badges inscribed "*za otlichie*" which these regiments previously had [147].

5 May 1833 - The **numbers** on headdress plates are ordered to be fixed on and not cut out [*ne proreznyi, a nakladnyi*]: of brass for lower ranks and gilt [*vyzolochennyi*] for officers [148].

15 April 1834 - **Cartridge pouches** [*lyadunki*]and **crossbelts** [*perevyazi*] are to be of the new pattern, with smaller-sized cover flaps [*kryshki*] and narrower crossbelts [149].

2 May 1834 - In order that **sabers** [*sabli*] may be better handled, it is ordered that their hilts [*yefesy*] be reworked according to a new pattern, as explained above for Dragoon regiments [150].

3 December 1834 - It is ordered that for all Lancer regiments each man have a **pistol**, carried on his person in a special holder [*chushka*] [151].

4 January 1835 - Gloves [*perchatki*] are ordered to be introduced for use by privates, of bluish-grey cloth and made from worn out riding trousers, and worn only at such times as when cloth mittens [*rukavitsy*] are worn in infantry forces; non-commissioned officers keep their deerskin gloves as before [152].

15 January 1835 - As a supplement to the above directive of 3 December 1834, all mounted trumpeters, non-commissioned officers, and privates are ordered to have one **pistol** each [153].

26 April 1835 - The following Lancer regiments are directed to have **numbers** on their headdress plates and buttons according to a new scheme: Voznesensk - 7, Olviopol - 8, Bug - 9, Odessa - 10, Orenburg - 11, Siberia - 12 [154].

15 July 1835 - The following regiments, which have a uniform **collar** the same color as the coat, are ordered to have piping on the top and sides of the collar, in the facing color: in the Ukraine, Novo-Arkhangelsk, Novo-Mirgorod, and Yelisavetgrad regiments - red; in the Duke of Nassau's (formerly the Lithuania) and Voznesensk - yellow; in the Volhynia and Olviopol - light blue; in the Bug and Orenburg - orange; and in the Odessa and Siberia - white [155].

19 July 1835 - To carry the pistol, it is ordered to have a **holder** [*chushka*] on the left side of the swordbelt [*portupeya*], as described above for Dragoon regiments [156].

10 November 1835 - It is directed to have chestnut **horses** in the Bug Lancer Regiment instead of greys, and greys in the Odessa Regiment instead of chestnuts [157].

31 January 1836 - Lower ranks' **greatcoats** are to have nine buttons instead of ten, as related above for Grenadier regiments [158].

27 April 1836 - **Lower pompons** [*repeiki*] are ordered to be backed with black leather [159].

13 May 1836 - Officers' **saddle girths** [*podprugi*] are to be dark green with red stripes [160].

9 October 1836 - As a place for their pistols, staff-trumpeters and trumpeters [*shtab-trubachi i trubachi*] are to have **holders** [*chushki*] of a special pattern, fitted to the saddle on the left side over the saddlecloth. And for cartridges they are to have **cartridge pouches** [*lyadunki*] with crossbelts, as for other lower ranks (Illus. 312) [161].

17 January 1837 - Confirmation is given to the directive regarding wearing the **saber** with the **frock coat**, as laid out above for Dragoon regiments [162].

14 February 1837 - Staff-trumpeters and trumpeters, who are prescribed pistols when in mounted formation and, for their cartridges, **cartridge pouches** [*lyadunki*] with belts, are also to wear these cartridgepouches when in dismounted formation [163].

11 March 1837 - Lancer regiments are ordered to have **carbines** [*karabiny*] of the same pattern as those introduced at this time in Dragoon and Hussar regiments [164].

13 July 1837 - With the introduction of new-pattern carbines in Lancer regiments, **swordbelts** for the carrying of sabers while in dismounted formation are directed to have brass hooks on straps with brass buckles, following the pattern for hussar swordbelts [165].

15 July 1837 - A new pattern of officers' **sash** [*sharf*] is approved, identical with that described above for Grenadier regiments [166].

14 August 1837 - Officers and lower ranks in formation are ordered to not pass their **headdress cords** [*etishkety*] under the epaulette, but simply wear them around the neck so that they hang to the middle of the back and fasten to the button on the headdress. Officers not in formation, and lower ranks in half-dress uniform [*poluforma*] are directed to wear the cords as before, passing them under the epaulette on the right shoulder [167].

17 August 1837 - With the directive that when the St.-Petersburg Lancer Regiment is in formation it is to have the silver **kettledrums** [*litavry*] granted to it in the Seven Years' War, these kettledrums are given banners [*zanavesy*] in the same color as the collar, trimmed in silver, while the kettledrummer [*litavrshchik*] is given a uniform with drum-major appointments [168].

17 December 1837 - A new pattern of officers' **epaulettes** is confirmed, identical with that introduced at this time in Dragoon regiments, i.e. with an additional, fourth, row of narrow braid [169].

11 January 1838 - Approval is given to the description of the officer's **saddle** which was prescribed for use on 6 March 1834, in agreement in all details with those presented above for Dragoon regiments [170].

23 February 1838 - Regulations are confirmed concerning the **pistol holders** [*pistoletnyya chushki*] mandated for the saddle on 9 October 1836, as set forth above for Dragoon regiments [171].

On this same date Highest confirmation is given to the following description of fitting **lancer headdress cords** [*ulanskii etishket*]:

"The line [*snur*] is fitted through the first slide [*gomba*], counting from above, when these cap cords [*etishket*] are fastened to the headdress, the ends of the line being passed through together and running alongside each other in parallel. In this way each end of the line is fitted through the 2nd, 3rd, 4th, and 5th slides, and the very ends, catching the upper loops of the bows [*banty*, i.e. the interwoven part above the fringed tassel, referred to in French as a *raquette* - M.C.], bend back upwards and are sewn fast, while above the slides the lines are sewn together in two places, leaving between the stitching an interval an inch in length, by which means a loop is created which fastens onto the top shoulder button [*na verkhnyuyu plechevuyu pugovitsu*]; the tassels [*kisti*] are put under the plastron so that they come out from under it towards the left shoulder and are seven inches above the third button. The lines near the end of the cap cord go to the back, having the 3rd slide behind the epaulette; the lines, making an opening between the 3rd and 2nd slides, are worn on the neck, and behind, at the collar seam at the middle of the back, the slides are drawn up one towards each other. The lines are let down on the back to the lower edge of the shoulder blade. Their ends go upwards and are fastened to the button up on top of the right side of the headdress.

"If the forage cap is worn, then the end of the lines go under the right shoulder and under the plastron and are fastened to the second button.

"A thin cord is tied to the upper end of the epaulette, about 14 inches long. On the coat, on the collar's lower seam, where the top of the epaulette should be, two reinforced holes [*obmetannyya diry*] are made, into which the ends of the thin cord are inserted and tied together on the inside. Small cross straps [*pogonchiki*] are sewn onto the shoulders: on the right shoulder both ends are sewn fast, but on the left shoulder the front end of this small strap is sewn fast while a small metal loop is sewn onto the other end. A loop of thread [*nityanaya petlya*] is made on the coat and from it, under the middle of the epaulette on the coat, is sewn a small wire hook. The small strap, going over the epaulette, is passed through the thread loop and fastened to this hook." [172]

17 April 1838 - In **HIS IMPERIAL HIGHNESS THE HEIR AND TSESAREVICH'S Lancer Regiment** (the former Courland) it is ordered that the collar and cuffs of officers' coats have embroidered silver lace-bars [*shityya serebryanyya petlitsy*] (Illus. 314) [173].

4 January 1839 - The **riding-trousers** [*reituzy*] of generals and field and company-grade officers are not to have any bows or bands in front [*speredi bantov ne imet*] but rather worn completely plain [*gladkii*] in the manner prescribed for lower ranks [174].

16 October 1840 - The regulation about lower ranks' silver **chevrons** [*shevrony*] is confirmed as laid out above for Grenadier regiments [175].

23 January 1841 - The capes [*bolshie vorotniki*] of officers' **greatcoats** are to be 28 inches long as measured from the bottom edge of the collar [176].

31 January 1843 - The **lances** [*piki*] in the regiments are to be reworked according to the new pattern, so that the shaft [*drevko*] with its point [*nakonechnik*] measures 10 ½ feet [177].

8 April 1843 - In the Voznesensk, Olviopol, Bug, and Odessa regiments the piping on the **riding trousers**, instead of being dark blue, is ordered to be the same color as the plastron, while the band on the **forage cap**, instead of being dark blue, is to be the color of the uniform headdress (Illus. 315). On this same date, in order to distinguish rank among the lower ranks, **lace** [*nashivki*] is to be sewn onto epaulettes and shoulder straps on the same basis as described above for Dragoon regiments, except that silver galloon is substituted for gold [178].

10 May 1843 - Regulations are prescribed for the size of cover flaps [*kryshki*] for **cartridge pouches** [*lyadunki*], for belt rings for **carbines**, and for the **belts** themselves, as set forth above for Dragoon regiments [179].

17 September 1843 - In **HIS IMPERIAL HIGHNESS THE GRAND DUKE NICHOLAS ALEKSANDROVICH'S Lancer Regiment** (the former Smolensk) it is ordered that the collar and cuffs of officers' coats [*mundiry*] have embroidered silver lace-bars (Illus. 316) [180].

2 January 1844 - Officers are to have a **cockade** on the band of the forage cap, as related above for Grenadier regiments [181].

19 February 1844 - A directive is issued for shortening the **bandolier** [*pantaler*] as set forth above for Dragoon regiments [182].

1844 May 20 - A new scheme for the various **forage caps** of lower ranks is confirmed, based on which they remain dark blue [*temnosinii*] as before, while the piping around the top is to be: in the 1st double-squadron [*divizion*] — red, in the 2nd — white, in the 3rd — light blue, in the 4th - blue [*sinii*], in the 5th - yellow, and in the reserve [*rezervnyi*] and replacement [*zapasnyi*] squadrons — dark green. The cap band is prescribed to be the same color as the uniform headdress, with two dark-blue pipings around both edges, and with the cut-out number of the squadron and the Cyrillic letter Е [for *eskadron* — M.C.]. When the cap band is orange or yellow, the numeral and letter are to be on red cloth, and for other colors they are to be on yellow. For officers of all double-squadrons the cap band is the same as for lower ranks, with two dark-blue pipings, but without numerals or letters, while the piping around the top of the forage cap is the same color as the band [183].

21 September 1844 - **Non-commissioned officer standard-bearers** [*shtandartnye unter-ofitsery*] in formation are to always have the cartridge pouch under the crossbelt for the standard [184].

15 November 1845 - All regiments are to have **pioneer axes** [*shantsovye topory*], two for each platoon [*vzvod*]. Additionally, there are to be 56 iron **spades** [*lopaty*] in each regiment [185].

19 November 1845 - On the **lances**, the clamps [*skoby*] which come out of the sharp upper end and blunt lower end to hold them to the shaft, as well as the small "ears" [*ushki*] in which the lance sling [*temlyak*] goes, are to be painted the same color as the shafts, as was done on the lances of the previous pattern [186].

13 September 1846 - Officers' **pistols** are to be of the new pattern with a percussion lock [*udarnyi zamok*], for which new carriers [*kobury*] are approved, made to fit these locks, as related in detail above for Army Cuirassier regiments [187].

28 December 1846 - With the naming of **HER IMPERIAL HIGHNESS THE GRAND DUCHESS CATHERINE MIKHAILOVNA** as Honorary Colonel [*Shef*, from the French *Chef* - M.C.] of the Serpukhov Lancer Regiment, it is ordered by Highest Authority that the collar and cuffs of officers' coats [*kolety*] in this reg. have silver lace-bars (Illus. 317) [188].

19 May 1847 - With the new general directive concerning the colors for **forage caps** within the War Department [*Voennoe vedomstvo*, i.e. the entire army — M.C.], the clerks, medics, and other lower ranks of Army Lancer regiments with dark-green forage caps are to have cap bands and piping around the top part in the same colors as the cap bands and piping of combatant lower ranks. However, barbers, hospital orderlies, and others with grey forage caps are to have piping on both edges of the cap band and around the top in the same color as the regiment's facing cloth [189].

7 July 1847 - Regimental adjutants [*Polkovye adyutanty*] in mounted formation are to have horses of the color prescribed for the regiments, not forbidding whomever wishes, however, to also have grey horses [190].

29 September 1847 - With the naming of **HIS IMPERIAL HIGHNESS THE GRAND DUKE CONSTANTINE NIKOLAEVICH** as Honorary Colonel of the Volhynia Lancer Regiment, it is ordered by Highest Authority that the collar and cuffs of officers' coats [*kolety*] in this regiment have silver lace-bars (Illus. 318) [191].

19 January 1848 - With the introduction of officers' pistols with percussion locks, Highest Authority confirms the description of the **firing-cap pouch** [*kapsyulnaya sumochka*] worn with the cartridge pouch that is described in detail above for Army Cuirassier regiments [192].

25 April 1848 - The valise's flap [*klapan na chemodane*] with buttons is completely done away with [193].

7 November 1849 - In Lancer regiments **pompons** are ordered to be 10 inches in circumference [194].

24 December 1849 - The grips of the **gold swords** awarded for bravery are to be gold instead of wrapped with black lacquered leather [195].

5 March 1850 - **Bandoliers** for standards are ordered to be 4 3/8 inches wide, 4 ½ feet long, and lined with cloth as follows:

For Archduke Carl-Ferdinand of Austria's Regiment - red on the outside and inside; fringes, galloon, and the hook with bracket are silver.

For the Chuguev Regiment - white on the outside, red on the inside; fringes, galloon, and the hook with bracket are silver.

For Prince Alexander of Hesse's Regiment - yellow on the outside, red on the inside; fringes, galloon, and the hook with bracket are silver.

For HER IMPERIAL HIGHNESS THE GRAND DUCHESS CATHERINE MIKHAILOVNA'S Regiment - light blue on the outside, red on the inside; fringes, galloon, and the hook with bracket are silver.

For His Imperial Highness Archduke Leopold of Austria's Regiment - red on the outside and inside; fringes, galloon, and the hook with bracket are silver.

For the Novo-Arkhangelsk Reg. - white on the outside, red on the inside; fringes, galloon, and the hook with bracket are silver.

For the Novo-Mirgorod Reg. - yellow on the outside, red on the inside; fringes, galloon, and the hook with bracket are silver.

For the Yelisavetgrad Reg. - light blue on the outside, red on the inside; fringes, galloon, and the hook with bracket are silver.

For General-Adjutant Prince Chernyshev's Regiment - yellow on the outside and inside; fringes, galloon, and the hook with bracket are silver.

For HIS IMPERIAL HIGHNESS THE HEIR AND TSESAREVICH'S Regiment - light blue on the outside and inside; fringes, galloon, and the hook with bracket are silver.

For HIS IMPERIAL HIGHNESS THE GRAND DUKE NICHOLAS ALEKSANDROVICH'S Regiment - orange on the outside and inside; fringes, galloon, and the hook with bracket are silver.

For the Kharkov Regiment - white on the outside, and inside; fringes, galloon, and the hook with bracket are silver.

For Archduke Albert of Austria's Reg. - yellow on the outside and inside; fringes, galloon, and the hook with bracket are silver.

For HIS IMPERIAL HIGHNESS THE GRAND DUKE CONSTANTINE NIKOLAEVICH'S Regiment - light blue on the outside and inside; fringes, galloon, and the hook with bracket are silver.

For the Voznesensk Regiment - yellow on the outside and inside; fringes, galloon, and the hook with bracket are silver.

For the Olviopol Regiment - light blue on the outside and inside; fringes, galloon, and the hook with bracket are silver.

For the Bug Regiment - orange on the outside, and inside; fringes, galloon, and the hook with bracket are silver.

For the Duke of Nassau's Regiment - white on the outside and inside; fringes, galloon, and the hook with bracket are silver.

For the Orenburg Regiment - orange on the outside and inside; fringes, galloon, and the hook with bracket are silver.

For the Siberia Regiment - white on the outside, and inside; fringes, galloon, and the hook with bracket are silver.

For HIS IMPERIAL HIGHNESS THE GRAND DUKE MICHAEL NIKOLAEVICH'S Regiment - yellow on the outside and inside; fringes, galloon, and the hook with bracket are silver.

For His Royal Highness Prince Frederick of Württemberg's Regiment - light blue on the outside and inside; fringes, galloon, and the hook with bracket are silver [196].

3 February 1851 - Highest Authority directs that **covers** [*chekhly*] for lower ranks' headdresses be introduced in Army Lancer regiments. These covers are to be of two halves such that the back one fastens to the front one and thus allows the chin scales to be worn on the visor, in the style of the officers [197].

30 March 1851 - With the introduction of smaller **bandoliers** [*pantalery*] and **crossbelts** with a movable firing-cap pouch [*perevyazi s peredvizhnoyu kapsyulnoyu sumochkoyu*] fitted onto a small iron hook, approval is given to their description as presented above in detail for Army Cuirassier regiments [198].

15 April 1851 - Approval is given to the description for fitting straps to the **valise** for dismounted lower ranks and prescribed to also be in effect for personnel released on leave from Cavalry units, as laid out in detail above for Cuirassier regiments [199].

31 December 1851 - With the naming of **HER IMPERIAL HIGHNESS THE GRAND DUCHESS CATHERINE MIKHAILOVNA** as Honorary Colonel of the Yelisavetgrad Lancer Regiment, which consequently is titled the Lancer Regiment of Her Highness, its officers are ordered to have silver lace-bars on the collar and cuffs of the coat [*kolet*] [200].

3 January 1852 - The cases or coverings [*chekhly, ili nakladki*] introduced for Army Infantry on 8 July 1851 for the **firing nipples** [*sterzhni*] of percussion weapons are ordered to also be used on percussion firearms in Cavalry forces [201].

18 January 1852 - In the **uniforms** of the Lancer regiments: HIS IMPERIAL HIGHNESS THE GRAND DUKE NICHOLAS ALEKSANDROVICH'S, the Bug, and His Highness Archduke Carl-Ferdinand of Austria, it is ordered to replace the color orange with the color red, and subsequently these regiments have:

HIS IMPERIAL HIGHNESS THE GRAND DUKE NICHOLAS ALEKSANDROVICH'S - red collar, plastron, cuffs, turnbacks, piping, and headdresses; dark-blue [*sinii*] collar patch; red edging to the saddlecloth (Illus. 319).

Bug - red plastron, cuffs, turnbacks, piping, and headdresses; dark-blue [*sinii*] collar with red piping; red edging to the saddlecloth (Illus. 320).

His Highness Archduke Carl-Ferdinand of Austria's - red plastron, cuffs, turnbacks, piping, and headdresses; dark-blue collar with red piping and collar patch; red edging to the saddlecloth (Illus. 321).

The **pennons** of these regiments are to have a red upper half and white lower half (Illus. 319) [202].

21 February 1852 - For the regiments of the **Reserve Lancer Division**: His Imperial Highness Archduke Leopold of Austria's Lancers, the Novo-Arkhangelsk, the Novo-Mirgorod, and HER IMPERIAL HIGHNESS THE GRAND DUCHESS CATHERINE MIKHAILOVNA'S, it is directed that the dark-blue **collars** of coats and greatcoats be red with dark-blue piping (Illus. 322, 323, 324, and 325) [203].

16 July 1852 - Cases or coverings for the **firing nipples** of percussion weapons in Army Cavalry forces are to be according to the description confirmed for Cuirassier regiments [204].

13 August 1853 - Generals and field and company-grade officers of Lancer regiments, when in campaign uniform [*pokhodnaya forma*], are directed to buckle the **swordbelt** over the **frock coat** [205].

18 February 1854 - The regulation of 15 November 1853 concerning light-cavalry **horse furniture**, presented above in the section for Army Cuirassier regiments, is also extended to Lancer regiments [206].

29 April 1854 - During wartime, generals and field and company-grade officers are to have **campaign greatcoats** [*pokhodnyya shineli*] of the same color and pattern as the greatcoats of lower ranks (Illus. 326), as described above for Grenadier regiments and following the same rules. With these greatcoats it is prescribed that there be worn swordbelts and pouchbelts of galloon in the same color as the buttons, while headdress cords and sashes are not to worn [207].

NOTES TO THE ILLUSTRATIONS

By Mark Conrad

277. In 1825 lancer uniforms were dark blue (coat, pants, and saddlecloth). The plastron, cuffs, piping, stripes on the girdle, as well as the saddlecloth's piping, stripe and monogram, were all in each regiment's distinctive color. All metal appointments were silver. The tufted ends of the other ranks' shoulder straps were white. On the headdress, the upper and lower pompons, band around the middle, cords, and edging on the upper part were white (silver for officers); the carrot-shaped part under the pompons, variously depicted by the Viskovatov artists, was the same color as the upper part of the headdress; the bottom part of the headdress was black, as was the flat top. The center stripe and edges of the

girdle were dark blue. Officers and non-commissioned officers wore white gloves, but lower ranks did not. The scabbard was steel; the sword hilt was brass. Lower ranks' sword knots were red leather, while for officers they were black with silver tassels. For lower ranks, the scabbard slings were red leather. The pouch belt was white (silver for officers, with a silver cartridge pouch with a gold double-headed eagle). The lance pennon's top was white, the bottom in the regiment's distinctive color; of the two stripes in the middle of the pennon, the upper was in the distinctive color and the lower was white. The lance strap was red leather.

Regiment.	Collar.	Upper half of headdress.	Distinctive color.	
Vladimir.	Red.	Red.	Red.	
Siberia.	Red.	White.	Red.	
Orenburg.	Red.	Yellow.	Red.	
Yamburg.	Red.	Light blue.	Red.	
1st Bug.	Dark blue.	Orange.	Orange.	
2nd Bug.	Dark blue.	White.	White.	
3rd Bug.	Dark blue.	Yellow.	Yellow.	
4th Bug.	Dark blue.	Light blue.	Light blue.	
Taganrog.	Dark blue.	Red.	Red.	
Chuguev.	Dark blue.	White.	Red.	
Borisoglebsk.	Dark blue.	Yellow.	Red.	
Serpukhov.	Dark blue.	Light blue.	Red.	(raspberry patch.)
Tatar.	Dark blue,	White.	White.	(white patch.)
Lithuania.	Dark blue,	Yellow.	Yellow.	(yellow patch.)
Volhynia.	Dark blue,	Light blue.	Light blue.	(light-blue patch.)
1st Ukraine.	Orange.	Orange.	Orange.	
2nd Ukraine.	White.	White.	White.	
3rd Ukraine.	Yellow.	Yellow.	Yellow.	
4th Ukraine.	Light blue.	Light blue.	Light blue.	

The Taganrog Regiment was renamed the Belgorod on 13 March 1826. At the rear of the saddle, there is a white sack for forage in front of the grey valise. The lower part of the surcingle is grey, the rest black. The bosses on the horse's forehead and chest are blackened. There is a grey greatcoat rolled under the front of the saddle-cloth.

278. The non-commissioned officer's lace around the collar and cuffs is silver.

279. Trumpeters' lace was white. Pants for other ranks were reinforced with black leather on the inside of the legs.

280. Officers' sashes were silver with orange and black checks interwoven in three lines. For officers' saddlecloths, the monogram was silver. The peaks of officers' headdresses were edged in silver.

283. On the staff-trumpeter's collar, the top lace is silver non-commissioned officers' tape, while the bottom of the collar has plain white musicians' lace. The base color of the swallows' nests on the staff-trumpeter's shoulders is red. There is white lace on the inside edge of the turnback. The non-commissioned officers' lower pompon has the mixed black/orange hourglass shape denoting his rank.

284. The prickers, chains, and rosette on the silver officer's pouch belt are also silver. Officers pants do not have leather reinforcement.

286. Brass trumpet with white cords.

287. The tracery on the bottom of the pants stripes may be unique to this regiment.

288. The shabraque for this regiment was of black sheep's fleece; the monogram in the corner was silver.

289. The outer crescents of the shoulder straps are in the facing color.

293. Dark-blue frock coat with red collar and red piping on the cuffs.

295. Brass plate on the cartridge pouch.

296. Black sheep's fleece shabraque.

312. Yellow chevrons on the upper sleeve. Grey horse.

323. Greatcoat collars are the same as on the coat.

Special thanks to Mr. Rob Thomas of Milwaukee, Wisconsin, for sharing his color photographs of a selection of Viskovatov's hand-colored plates, obtained with great effort from a special Imperial edition of this work held in Russia.

9. HUSSAR REGIMENTS (*GUSARKIE POLKI*).

11 February 1826 - Clerks and in general all non-combatant lower ranks are ordered to have grey **riding trousers** [*reituzy*] with stripes [*lampasy*] [208].

10 June 1826 - *Chakchiry* pants and high boots are withdrawn, and it is ordered to always wear grey cloth **riding trousers** without stripes, with only one line of piping on the side seam [209].

15 September 1826 - Lower ranks who have served out the regulation number of years without reproach and who voluntarily remain on service are ordered to wear **gold galloon** sewn onto the left sleeve, as related above for Cuirassier regiments [210].

25 November 1826 - There are the following **changes in uniforms** for Hussar regiments:

1.) In all regiments the collar and cuffs are to be the same color as the dolman [*doloman*].

2.) Buttons on the pelisse [*mentik*] and dolman are to be in three rows.

3.) The fleece trim [*opushka*] on the pelisse is to be black.

4.) Riding trousers are to be made from bluish-grey cloth, with piping on the side seams in the same color as the shako.

5.) Shakos [*kivera*] are to be higher than before, in the style confirmed on 9 February 1828 for Dragoon and Horse-Jäger regiments but in various colors according to the listing below.

6.) On girdles [*kushaki*] [sometimes called "barrel sashes" in English - M.C.] the tassels are to be the same color as the braid, but the slides [*gomby*] are the color of the shako.

7.) Forage caps are to be the same color as the dolman, with bands according to the regiment's distinctive color.

8.) For all regiments, the collars and cuffs of officers' undress coats [*vitse-mundiry*] are to dark green with colored piping. With this, the prescribed colors for regiments are as follows:

Sumy Regiment	red shako; grey pelisse and dolman; white buttons, braid [*snury*], and shako cords [*vitishkety*]; red sabertache [*tashka*] with white trim, monogram, and crown; grey saddle cloth [*val'trap*] with white trim, monogram, and crown; red piping on officers' undress coats (Illus. 327).
Olviopol Regiment	red shako; olive [*olivkovyi*] pelisse and dolman; white buttons, braid, and shako cords; red sabertache with white trim, monogram, and crown; olive saddle cloth with white trim, monogram, and crown; olive piping on officers' undress coats (Illus. 328).
Klyastitsy Regiment	light-blue [*svetlosinii*] shako; blue [*sinii*] pelisse and dolman; white buttons, braid, and shako cords; white sabertache with light-blue trim, monogram, and crown; blue saddle cloth with white trim, monogram, and crown; light-blue piping on officers' undress coats (Illus. 329).
Lubny Regiment	yellow shako; blue pelisse and dolman; white buttons, braid, and shako cords; yellow sabertache with white trim, monogram, and crown; blue saddle cloth with white trim, monogram, and crown; yellow piping on officers' undress coats (Illus. 329).
Archduke Ferdinand's Regiment (formerly the Izyum)	red shako; blue pelisse; red dolman; yellow buttons; white braid and shako cords; red sabertache with white trim, monogram, and crown; blue saddle cloth with white trim, monogram, and crown; red piping on officers' undress coats (Illus. 330).
Pavlograd Regiment	turquoise [*biryuzovyi*] shako and pelisse; dark-green dolman; yellow buttons, braid, and shako cords; turquoise sabertache with yellow trim, monogram, and crown; dark-green saddle cloth with yellow trim, monogram, and crown; turquoise piping on officers' undress coats (Illus. 331).
Yelisavetgrad Regiment	grey shako, pelisse, and dolman; yellow buttons, braid, and shako cords; grey sabertache and saddle cloth, with yellow trim, monogram, and crown; grey piping on officers' undress coats (Illus. 332).
Irkutsk Regiment	raspberry [*malinovyi*] shako; black pelisse and dolman; yellow buttons, braid, and shako cords; raspberry sabertache with yellow trim, monogram, and crown; black saddle cloth with yellow trim, monogram, and crown; raspberry piping on officers' undress coats (Illus. 333).
Akhtyrka Regiment	yellow shako; brown pelisse and dolman; yellow buttons, braid, and shako cords; yellow sabertache with brown trim, monogram, and crown; brown saddle cloth with yellow trim, monogram, and crown; brown piping on officers' undress coats (Illus. 334).
Aleksandriya Regiment	red shako; black pelisse and dolman; white buttons, braid, and shako cords; red sabertache with white trim, monogram, and crown; black saddle cloth with white trim, monogram, and crown; black piping on officers' undress coats (Illus. 334).

Field Marshal Graf Wittgenstein's Regiment	yellow shako; blue pelisse and dolman; yellow buttons; white braid and shako cords; yellow sabertache with blue trim, monogram, and crown; blue saddle cloth with yellow trim, monogram, and crown; yellow piping on officers' undress coats (Illus. 334).
The Prince of Orange's Regiment	light-blue shako and dolman; red pelisse; white buttons, braid, and shako cords; light-blue sabertache and saddle cloth, with white trim, monogram, and crown; green piping on officers' undress coats (Illus. 335).
Ingermanland Regiment	light-blue shako, pelisse, and dolman; yellow buttons, braid, and shako cords; light-blue sabertache and saddle cloth, with yellow trim, monogram, and crown; light-blue piping on officers' undress coats (Illus. 335).
Narva Regiment	light-blue shako, pelisse, and dolman; white buttons, braid, and shako cords; light-blue sabertache and saddle cloth, with white trim, monogram, and crown; white piping on officers' undress coats (Illus. 335).
Kiev Regiment	raspberry shako; olive pelisse and dolman; yellow buttons, braid, and shako cords; raspberry sabertache with yellow trim, monogram, and crown; olive saddle cloth with yellow trim, monogram, and crown; olive piping on officers' undress coats (Illus. 336).
Mitau Regiment	yellow shako; turquoise pelisse and dolman; white buttons, braid, and shako cords; yellow sabertache with white trim, monogram, and crown; turquoise saddle cloth with white trim, monogram, and crown; turquoise piping on officers' undress coats (Illus. 336) [211].

1 January 1827 - In order to distinguish rank, it is ordered that officers' **epaulettes** (on the undress coat) are to have small forged and stamped stars of the same appearance and according to the same scheme as related above for Grenadier regiments [212].

17 February 1827 - Officers' **girdles** [*poyasy*] are directed to have a mixture of black and orange silk (Illus. 337) [213].

22 July 1827 - Instead of cloaks [*plashchi*] it is ordered to have **greatcoats** [*shineli*] with dark-green collars piped on the top and front edges in the same color as the piping on officers' undress coats (Illus. 338) [214].

31 July 1827 - Numbers and letters on **shako covers** [*kivernye chekhly*] are directed to be in yellow oil paints [215].

13 October 1827 - On their undress coats, generals and field and company-grade officers are to have **epaulettes** with a scaled field [*epolety s cheshuichatym polem*], as established at this time for Dragoon and Horse-Jäger regiments [216].

11 December 1827 - For the Prince of Orange's and Archduke Ferdinand's regiments, the collars and cuffs of **undress coats** are ordered to have embroidery [*vyshivka*] of the same style as in the L.-Gds. Hussar Regiment: silver in the first regiment and gold in the second (Illus. 339) [217].

14 December 1827 - The **lace** [*nashivka*] sewn onto lower ranks' left sleeves, instituted on 15 September 1826, is to be gold or silver according to the color of the buttons, and of the non-commissioned officers' galloon used by the regiment in which the man voluntarily remains in service after serving out the regulation number of years for retirement [218].

22 February 1828 - It is ordered to have **shoulder straps** on lower ranks' greatcoats in the same color as the shako (Illus. 340) [219].

7 March 1828 - Lower ranks who return to their regiments from the Model Cavalry Regiment, as well as those who have previously been in the Instructional Cavalry Squadron, are to have yellow tape trimmed with red sewn onto the **shoulder straps** of the greatcoat [*imet' na pogonakh shinelei nashivki, iz zheltago s krasnym basona*], as described in detail for Grenadier regiments. The same tape is also ordered to be on the shoulder cords [*plechevyya snurki*] of pelisses and dolmans [220].

24 March 1828 - The **dolmans** of lower ranks are forbidden to have cinches [*peretyazhki*] [221].

24 April 1828 - All non-combatants of non-commissioned officer rank are given dark-green **frock coats** [*syurtuki*] with one row of buttons [*odnobortnyi*] in place of the grey coats [*mundiry*] they were using. These have the same collar and cuffs as before and piping and shoulder straps the same color as the shako, while in contrast to combatant ranks the pants are grey, with piping down the side seams. Non-combatant master-craftsmen in the lower ranks, as well as infirmary orderlies, are ordered to wear **jackets** [*kurtki*] in place of the coats they previously used. These are of grey cloth, as before, and pants are as for the preceding non-combatants [222].

3 November 1828 - Tassels on musicians' **trumpets** are directed to be the same color as the braid on the uniform, but in regiments with St.-George trumpets they are to be in the colors of St.-George ribbon [i.e., orange and black - M.C.] [223].

20 December 1828 - Shakos are given new pattern **plates**, the same as those established on 24 April 1828 for Infantry and Jäger regiments, i.e. with cut-out figures of the regiment's assigned number (Illus. 341). These plates are of the same color as before, i.e. yellow or white according to the color of the buttons. Numbers are as follows: in the Sumy Regiment - *1*, Olviopol - *2*, Klyastitsy - *3*, Lubny - *4*, Archduke Ferdinand's - *5*, Pavlograd - *6*, Yelisavetgrad - *7*, Irkutsk - *8*, Akhtyrka - *9*, Aleksandriya - *10*, Field Marshal Graf Wittgenstein's - *11*, The Prince of Orange's - *12*, Ingermanland - *13*, Narva - *14*, Kiev - *15*, and Mitau - *16*. The Sumy, Klyastitsy, Lubny, Archduke Ferdinand's, Pavlograd, Yelisavetgrad, and Kiev regiments are ordered to have infantry-pattern badges with the inscription "*Za otlichie*" ["For excellence"], and badges inscribed "*Za otlichie 14 Avgusta 1813 goda*" ["For distinction, 14 August 1813"] are to be for the Akhtyrka, Aleksandriya, Graf Wittgenstein's, and the Prince of Orange's regiments [224].

16 December 1829 - Instead of being colored, the cuffs of officers' **frock coats** [*syurtuki*] are to be the same color as the frock, with piping of the same color as the piping on the undress coat. On 26 December, all combatant ranks are ordered to have uniform buttons with the raised image of the number prescribed for the shako plate [225].

15 April 1830 - The lining on the tails and turnbacks [*obkladki pol i fald*] of officers' **undress coats**, instead of being red, is to be the same color as the coat - dark green, and with piping the same color as the piping on the collar. The lining [*podboi*] under the turnbacks is also to be dark green (Illus. 342) [226].

24 September 1830 - The lining [*podkladka*] of officers' **frock coats** is to be dark green like the color of the frock coat itself [227].

1 January 1832 - Generals possessing **gold sabers** decorated with diamonds and inscribed "*Za Khrabost*" ["For Courage"] are ordered to wear these without swordknots [228].

18 October 1832 - Officers' **undress coats** in HIS IMPERIAL HIGHNESS THE GRAND DUKE MICHAEL PAVLOVICH'S Hussar Regiment (formerly the Narva Regiment) are to have light-blue piping instead of white (Illus. 343) [229].

3 January 1833 - **Covers for shakos** are discontinued [230].

20 January 1833 - These **covers for shakos** are kept as before [231].

22 February 1833 - Field and company-grade officers are ordered to not wear hats, but rather always be in **shakos** [232].

21 March 1833 - Hussar regiments are directed to have **numbers** on their buttons and shako plates, and **horses**, as follows: for the *Sumy* - number 1, chestnut [*gnedye*] horses; *Klyastitsy* - number 2, grey horses; *Yelisavetgrad* - number 3, sorrel [*ryzhie*] horses; *Lubny* - number 4, black [*voronye*] horses, with bays [*karie*] and dark chestnuts [*temnognedye*] allowed to be included; *Field Marshal Graf Wittgenstein's* - number 5, chestnut horses; *Prince of Orange's* - number 6, grey horses; *Kiev* - number 7, sorrel horses; *Ingermanland* - number 8, black horses, with bays and dark chestnuts allowed to be included; *Pavlograd* - number 9, chestnut horses; *Archduke Ferdinand's* - number 10, grey horses; *Akhtyrka* - number 11, sorrel horses; *Aleksandriya* - number 12, black horses, with bays and dark chestnuts allowed to be included; *HIS IMPERIAL HIGHNESS THE GRAND DUKE MICHAEL PAVLOVICH'S* - number 13, chestnut horses; *His Majesty the King of Württemberg's* (formerly the Mitau) - number 14, grey horses [233].

5 May 1833 - The figures or **numbers** on shako plates are ordered to be fixed on and not cut out: of tin on brass plates (silver for officers), and of brass on white plates (gold for officers) (Illus. 344) [234].

26 February 1834 - The **Kiev Hussar Regiment** is ordered to have red shakos; dark-green pelisses and dolmans; yellow shako cords, lace, and braid; blue-grey riding trousers with red piping; yellow girdles with red slides; red sabertaches with yellow trim, monogram, and crown; dark-green saddle cloths with yellow trim, monogram, and crown; dark-green collar and cuffs on officers' undress coats, with red piping; yellow buttons on greatcoats, pelisses, and dolmans, with the number 7 (Illus. 345). **His Majesty the King of Württemberg's Hussar Regiment** is ordered to have yellow shakos; dark-green pelisses and dolmans; white shako cords, lace, and braid; blue-grey riding trousers with yellow piping; white girdles with yellow slides; yellow sabertaches with white trim, monogram, and crown; dark-green saddle cloths with white trim, monogram, and crown; dark-green collar and cuffs on officers' undress coats, with yellow piping; white buttons with the number 14 (Illus. 346). In both regiments the fleece trim on the pelisse is black. The collar and cuffs on the dolman are the same color as the rest of the dolman; buttons on the pelisse and dolman, for officers as well as lower ranks, are in three rows. Dark-green collar on the greatcoat; dark-green piping on the collar, while shoulder straps are the color of the shako. Lower ranks of the Kiev Regiment are to have yellow worsted trim [*pribor*], but gold for officers; lower ranks of the King of Württemberg's Regiment are to have white trim, and officers - silver [235].

13 April 1834 - **Cartridge pouches** [*lyadunki*] and **crossbelts** [*perevyazi*] are to be of the new pattern, with smaller-sized cover flaps [*kryshki*] and narrower crossbelts [236].

2 May 1834 - In order that **sabers** [*sabli*] may be better handled, it is ordered that their hilts [*yefesy*] be reworked according to a new pattern, so that the straight arch, where it joins the headpiece, is sawn off even with the curving part, while the small flat part on the grip's brass trim, and this trim itself where it is pressed by the thumb, are to be cut smooth [237].

3 December 1834 - It is ordered that there be no **pistols** in Hussar regiments [238].

7 December 1834 - Lines to the **shako** (when this is worn) are not to reach to the waist, as before, but only halfway down the back [239].

4 January 1835 - **Gloves** [*perchatki*] are directed to be taken into use by privates [*ryadovye*], of bluish-grey cloth and made from worn-out riding trousers, and worn only at such times as when cloth mittens [*rukavitsy*] are worn in infantry forces; non-commissioned officers keep their deerskin gloves as before [240].

15 January 1835 - Mounted non-commissioned officers are ordered to have one **pistol** each [241].

20 January 1835 - With the withdrawal of pistols from Hussar regiments, the **ramrods** [*shompoly*] that used to be on the cartridge pouches are also discontinued. Along with this, a new pattern of **bandolier**, or shoulder belt, [*pantaler ili pogonnaya perevyaz'*] is confirmed for Carabiniers, with brass fittings, iron hook, and ramrod strap [242].

13 April 1835 - Officers in formation are to have one end of the **shako lines** [*kivernyi shnur*] fastened with a toggle and loop behind the shako fashioned from the shako cord [*etishketnyi snur*], and at all other times, when officers are not in formation and must take off their shakos, these lines are unfastened from that loop and, leaving them around the neck with their slide (which must be in back at the middle of the neck), the end with the toggle is fastened to the undress coat's second button from the top, so that the lines pass under the right arm and over the pouch belt [243].

26 April 1835 - Hussar regiments are ordered to have **numbers** on their headdress plates and buttons according to a new scheme: Pavlograd - 7, Archduke Ferdinand's - 8, Akhtyrka - 9, Aleksandriya - 10, Kiev - 11, Ingermanland - 12 [244].

19 July 1835 - To carry the pistol, it is ordered to have a **holder** [*chushka*] on the left side of the swordbelt [*portupeya*], on the same basis as described above for Dragoon regiments. Beginning in this same year pelisses began to be worn over the back instead of on the left shoulder (Illus. 347) [245].

31 January 1836 - Lower ranks' **greatcoats** are to have nine buttons instead of ten, as related above for Grenadier regiments [246].

27 April 1836 - **Lower pompons** [*repeiki*] are ordered to be backed with black leather [247].

13 May 1836 - Officers' **saddle girths** [*podprugi*] are to be dark green with red stripes [248].

9 October 1836 - As a place for their pistols, staff-trumpeters and trumpeters are to have **holders** [*chushki*] of a special pattern, fitted to the saddle over the saddle cloth on the left side. And for cartridges they are to have **cartridge pouches** [*lyadunki*] with crossbelts, as for other lower ranks (Illus. 347) [249].

14 February 1837 - Staff-trumpeters and trumpeters, who are prescribed pistols when in mounted formation and, for cartridges, **cartridge pouches** with belts, are also to wear these cartridgepouches when in dismounted formation [250].

11 March 1837 - The muskets [*ruzh'ya*] in Hussar regiments are replaced with short **carbines** [*karabiny*] of the same pattern as those introduced at this time in Dragoon regiments [251].

17 December 1837 - A new pattern of officers' **epaulettes** (for the undress coat) is confirmed, identical with that introduced at this time in Dragoon regiments, i.e. with an additional, fourth, row of braid [252].

23 February 1838 - Regulations are confirmed concerning the **pistol holders** [*pistoletnyya chushki*] mandated for the saddle on 9 October 1836, as set forth above for Dragoon regiments [253].

21 May 1838 - New patterns are confirmed for the **pelisse** [*mentiya*] and **dolman**. The first of these is directed to be made so that it can be worn over the dolman with the sleeves hanging loose [*v rukava*] (Illus. 348) [254].

4 January 1839 - The **riding-trousers** [*reituzy*] of generals and field and company-grade officers are not to have any bows or bands in front [*speredi bantov ne imet'*] but rather worn completely plain [*gladkii*] in the manner prescribed for lower ranks [255].

25 February 1839 - Field and company-grade officers of Hussar regiments which have members of Imperial or Royal families, as well as foreign Princes, as Honorary Colonels [*Shefy*], are to have embroidered [*shityi*] collars and cuffs on **undress coats** of the same pattern as those prescribed for the undress coats of Guards Hussar regiments [256].

16 October 1840 - The regulation concerning lower ranks' gold **chevrons** [*shevrony*] is confirmed as laid out above for Grenadier regiments [257].

23 January 1841 - The capes [*bolshie vorotniki*] of officers' **greatcoats** are to be 28 inches long as measured from the bottom edge of the collar [258].

8 April 1843 - Officers and combatant lower ranks are given a new pattern **shako** [*kiver*] 8 1/4 inches high and curving inward a little toward the bottom (Illus. 349) [259]. Along with this, in order to distinguish rank among the lower ranks, it is ordered to have **shoulder cords** [*epoletnye shnurki*] with small slides [*gombochki*] on both shoulders of the pelisse as well as the dolman, according to the following scheme:

1.) *For senior sergeants [starshie vakhmistry]* - yellow woolen or white linen [*iz beli*] cord [*shnurok*], bent double, of the same style and color on both the pelisse and the dolman, with one gold or silver (according to the buttons) slide set near the shoulder seam (Illus. 350, a).

2.) *For distinguished officer candidates and officer candidates [portupei-yunkera i yunkera]* - narrow gold or silver (according to the buttons) braided cord [*pleteshek*], bent double, without any slide (Illus. 350, b).

3.) *For junior sergeants [mladshie vakhmistry]* - yellow woollen or white linen cord, bent double, of the same style and color on both the pelisse and the dolman, with three slides the same color as the cord (of wool or linen), each one set alongside the other, near the shoulder seam (Illus. 350, c).

4.) *For non-commissioned officers [unter-ofitsery]* - the same style cord in the same colors, with two slides the same color as the cord (Illus. 350, d).

5.) *For corporals [yefreitory]* - the same style cord in the same colors, with one slide the same color as the cord (Illus. 350, e). Shoulder straps on the greatcoat are to have galloon or tape sewn on following the same scheme as described above for Grenadier and Cuirassier regiments [260].

10 May 1843 - Cover flaps [*kryshki*] for **cartridge pouches** [*lyadunki*] are to be (with the cover sewn to the box): 8 inches long, 9 inches wide at the top edge, and 10 inches wide along the bottom edge. The oval belt rings for **carbines** are to be replaced with circular ones. Belts are attached to the stocks of the carbines by means of special straps with buckles, and in order to avoid the upper brass band hitting the spurs, as well as so that the carbines do not drag on the ground when dismounted, they are to be raised up by shortening the bandolier, according to the height of the individual [261].

2 June 1843 - Rules for fixing plates and badges for distinction to the **shako** are confirmed, the same as set forth above for Grenadier regiments [262].

2 January 1844 - Officers are to have a **cockade** on the cap band of the forage cap, as related above for Grenadier regiments [263].

19 February 1844 - The shortening of the **bandolier** according to the height of the soldier, as laid down on 10 May 1843, is ordered to be done using the brass buckle at its end so that its lower end is even with the lower edge of the dolman [264].

1844 May 20 - A new scheme for the different **forage caps** of lower ranks is confirmed, based on which they are ordered to be the same color as the dolman, with piping around the top edge to be: in the 1st double-squadron [*divizion*] — red, in the 2nd — white, in the 3rd — light blue, in the 4th - blue, and in the reserve [*rezervnyi*] and replacement [*zapasnyi*] squadrons — dark green. The cap band is prescribed to be the same color as the shako, with piping around the edges according to the color of the buttons: of yellow cloth for brass buttons and white for tin. The band also has the cut-out number of the squadron and the Cyrillic letter "*E*" [for *eskadron* — M.C.]. When the cap band is yellow, the numeral and letter are to be on red cloth, and for other colors they are to be on yellow. For officers of all double-squadrons the cap band is the same as for lower ranks and with the same piping, but without numerals or letters, while the piping around the top of the forage cap is the same color as the piping on the band [265].

21 September 1844 - **Non-commissioned officer standard-bearers** [*shtandartnye unter-ofitsery*] in formation are to always have the cartridge pouch under the crossbelt for the standard [266].

17 December 1844 - In order to distinguish **rank** between generals and field and company-grade officers, dolmans and pelisses are to have cords and slides [*shnurki i gombochki*] with small stars: silvered on gold slides, and gilt on silver ones, and following the number of small stars on the epaulettes (Illus. 351) [267].

10 January 1845 - HER IMPERIAL HIGHNESS THE GRAND DUCHESS OLGA NIKOLAEVNA's Hussar Regiment (the former Yelisavetgrad) is ordered to have: white shakos and pelisses, light-blue dolmans, white sabertaches, light-blue saddle cloths, white shoulder straps and collar piping on greatcoats, white piping on riding trousers, and yellow braid, lace, and trim on the uniform, as before (Illus. 352) [268].

26 February 1845 - Instead of the undress coats [*vitse-mundiry*] they were using, field and company-grade officers are ordered to have **jackets** [*kurtki*] the same color as the dolman, trimmed with gold or silver cord [*shnurki*], as well as galloon for field-grade officers, according to the color of the cord and galloon on pelisses and dolmans. Riding trousers worn with these jackets are kept the same as before, of blue-grey cloth (Illus. 353). Generals in hussar uniforms are also allowed to wear such jackets on those occasions when the undress coat was worn. This **undress coat** was then kept only for generals [269].

18 August 1845 - With the newly introduced jackets, officers on campaign [*vo fronte*] are ordered to have the **sabertache** in a cover [*chekhol*], and instead of frock coats [*syurtuki*] they are given new-pattern ***vengerki* coats** [literally, "Hungarians" - M.C.] (Illus. 354). Generals are allowed to wear the previous undress coats and frocks [270].

8 September 1845 - With the **jacket** introduced on 26 February 1845, officers on duty and holding official positions [*na dezhurstvakh i v dolzhnostyakh*] are ordered to wear the cartridge pouch, girdle, and sabertache in case [271].

15 November 1845 - All regiments are ordered to have **pioneer axes** [*shantsovye topory*], two in each platoon, plus 56 iron **shovels** [*lopaty*] in each regiment, as mentioned above for Cuirassier regiments [272].

13 September 1846 - Officers' **pistols** are to be of the new pattern with a percussion lock [*udarnyi zamok*], for which new carriers [*kobury*] are approved, made to fit these locks [273].

26 October 1846 - The collars on **generals' uniform coats** [*mundiry*] are ordered to be open [*razreznyi*] [274].

19 May 1847 - With the new general directive concerning the colors for **forage caps** within the War Department [*Voennoe vedomstvo*, i.e. the entire army — M.C.], the clerks, medics, and other lower ranks of Army Hussar regiments with dark-green forage caps are to have cap bands in the same color as the caps, and piping around the top in the same color as the shakos of combatant ranks. However, barbers, hospital orderlies, and others with grey forage caps are to have piping on both edges of the cap band and around the top in the same color as the regiment's facing cloth [275].

7 July 1847 - **Regimental adjutants** [*Polkovye adyutanty*] in mounted formation are to have horses of the color prescribed for the regiments, not forbidding whomever wishes, however, to also have grey horses [276].

19 January 1848 - With the introduction of officers' pistols with percussion locks, Highest Authority confirms the description of the **firing-cap pouch** [*kapsyulnaya sumochka*] worn with the cartridge pouch that is described in detail above for Army Cuirassier regiments [277].

25 April 1848 - The **valise's flap** [*klapan na chemodane*] with buttons is completely done away with [278].

7 November 1849 - In Hussar regiments **pompons** are ordered to be 10 inches in circumference [279].

17 December 1849 - The **greatcoats** in Army Hussar regiments, both for officers and lower ranks, are to have: *collar* - the same color as the dolman; *piping* around the collar - yellow or white, according to the color of the appointments, but white in Archduke Ferdinand's Hussar Regiment; *shoulder straps* for lower ranks - the same color as the shako (Illus. 355) [280].

24 December 1849 - The grips of the **gold swords** awarded for bravery are to be gold instead of wrapped with black lacquered leather [281].

5 March 1850 - **Bandoliers** for standards are ordered to be 4 3/8 inches wide, 4 1/2 feet long, and lined with cloth as follows:

For the Sumy Reg. - red on the outside and grey-blue on the inside; fringes, galloon, and the hook with bracket are silver.

For the Klyastitsy Reg. - light-blue on the outside, blue on the inside; fringes, galloon, and the hook with bracket are silver.

For HER IMPERIAL HIGHNESS THE GRAND DUCHESS OLGA NIKOLAEVNA'S Regiment - white on the outside and inside; fringes, galloon, and the hook with bracket are gold.

For His Majesty the King of Hannover's Regiment - yellow on the outside, blue on the inside; fringes, galloon, and the hook with bracket are silver.

For Prince Frederick of Hesse-Kassel's Regiment - yellow on the outside, blue on the inside; fringes, galloon, and the hook with bracket are gold.

For His Majesty the King of the Netherlands' Regiment - light blue on the outside, red on the inside; fringes, galloon, and the hook with bracket are silver.

For His Imperial Highness the Heir and Tsesarevich's Regiment - turquoise on the outside and inside; fringes, galloon, and the hook with bracket are gold.

For Archduke Ferdinand's Regiment - red on the outside and inside; fringes, galloon, and the hook with bracket are gold.

For the Akhtyrka Reg. - yellow on the outside, brown on the inside; fringes, galloon, and the hook with bracket are gold.

For General-Field Marshal the Prince of Warsaw, Graf Paskevich of Erivan's Regiment - red on the outside, black on the inside; fringes, galloon, and the hook with bracket are silver.

For His Imperial Highness Duke Maximilian of Leuchtenberg's Regiment - red on the outside, dark green on the inside; fringes, galloon, and the hook with bracket are gold.

For the Hereditary Grand Duke of Saxe-Weimar's Regiment - light blue on the outside and inside; fringes, galloon, and the hook with bracket are gold.

For HIS IMPERIAL HIGHNESS THE GRAND DUKECONSTANTINE NIKOLAEVICH'S Regiment - light blue on the outside and inside; fringes, galloon, and the hook with bracket are silver.

For His Majesty the King of Württemberg's Regiment - yellow on the outside, dark green on the inside; fringes, galloon, and the hook with bracket are silver [282].

10 June 1850 - **Forage caps** in Archduke Ferdinand's Hussar Regiment (the former Izyum) are ordered to be of blue cloth with red bands that are piped yellow on both edges. The piping around the top of the cap, though, is left as previously confirmed on 20 May 1844 (Illus. 356), and namely:

For officers - the same color as the piping around the band - yellow.

For lower ranks:

In the 1st double-squadron [*divizion*] - red (Illus. 356).   In the 2nd double-squadron - white.

In the 3rd double-squadron - light blue.   In the 4th double-squadron - blue.

In the reserve [*rezervnyi*] and replacement [*zapasnyi*] double-squadrons - dark green [283].

30 March 1851 - With the introduction of smaller **bandoliers** and **crossbelts** with a movable firing-cap pouch fitted onto a small iron hook, approval is given to the description of them presented above in detail for Army Cuirassier regiments (Illus. 357) [284].

15 April 1851 - Approval is given to the description for fitting straps to the **valise** for dismounted lower ranks and prescribed to also be in effect for personnel released on leave from cavalry units, and laid out in detail above for Cuirassier reg. [285].

3 January 1852 - The cases or coverings [*chekhly, ili nakladki*] introduced for Army Infantry on 8 July 1851 for the **firing nipples** [*sterzhni*] of percussion weapons are ordered to also be used on percussion firearms in Cavalry forces [286].

14 June 1852 - In those Hussar regiments in which **pompons** are orange, it is ordered that they be close to the color of yellow cavalry facing cloth [*pod tsvet zheltago, pribornago, kavaleriiskago sukna*] [287].

12 July 1852 - Officers of His Royal Highness Prince Frederick-William of Prussia's Hussar Regiment, in order to achieve uniformity in dress, are ordered to wear red **jackets** instead of blue ones, at all those times when jackets were previously prescribed to be worn in this regiment. Additionally, they are to wear the red jackets when in camp uniform and on campaign [*pri lagernoi forme i vo fronte*] when lower ranks are in dolmans, i.e. in summer campaign dress, [288].

16 July 1852 - Cases or coverings for the **firing nipples** of percussion weapons in Army Cavalry forces are to be according to the description confirmed by Highest Authority on 8 July 1851 and set forth above for Cuirassier regiments [289].

29 August 1852 - In order to be distinguished from company-grade officers, field-grade officers in each regiment are ordered to have galloon on the collars of their *vengerki* and **jackets**, this galloon being of the newly confirmed pattern, similar to the galloon prescribed for their sleeves (Illus. 358) [290].

[**16 October - 3 November 1852** - Steps taken by the Commissariat Department regarding the introduction of new collars for **jackets** and *vengerki* of field-grade officers in hussar regiments. (RGVIA, f. 14940, op. 1-2 (shtab 4-go Armeiskago korpusa 1830-64), d. 414, 5 ll. 1082. 89-680) - M.C.]

3 January 1853 - Non-combatant lower ranks in Hussar regiments who up to now had dark-green **caps** with bands of that same color are ordered to have bands and piping of the same colors as prescribed for the forage caps of combatant lower ranks. The same bands and piping are prescribed for those non-combatant lower ranks who have grey caps [291].

13 August 1853 - Generals and field and company-grade officers, when in the campaign uniform [*pokhodnaya forma*] of a *vengerka* coat without girdle, are directed to buckle the **swordbelt** [*portupeya*] over the *vengerka* [292].

27 November 1853 - **General-Adjutant Graf von-der-Pahlen's Hussar Regiment** (the former Sumy) is prescribed the following uniform:

Red shako, of the previous pattern. Yellow shako cords. Yellow pompon. Brass shako plates, scales, badges of distinction, and buckles. Pelisse of light-blue cloth. Dolman of white cloth. Yellow braid and lace. Riding trousers of the previous pattern, with red piping. Yellow girdle, with red slides. Sabertache of red cloth, with trim and monogram of yellow cloth. Yellow braid. Saddle cloth of light-blue cloth, with yellow trim. White collar on the greatcoat, with yellow piping, while shoulder straps for lower ranks are red. White forage caps with a red band and yellow piping. White jackets for field and company-grade officers, and *vengerki* of light-blue cloth (Illus. 359, 360, 361, and 362) [293].

11 February 1854 - Highest Authority orders that general officers' **undress coats** in General-Adjutant Graf von-der-Pahlen's Hussar Regiment, in order to be distinguished from those in HIS IMPERIAL HIGHNESS THE GRAND DUKE NICHOLAS MAKSIMILIANOVICH'S Hussar Regiment, and in supplement to the changes of 27 November 1853, are to have light-blue piping instead of red, and red edging [*kant*] is left only on the riding trousers [294].

18 February 1854 - The regulation of 15 November 1853 concerning light-cavalry **horse furniture**, presented above in the section for Army Cuirassier regiments, is also extended to Hussar regiments [295].

29 April 1854 - During wartime, generals and field and company-grade officers are to have **campaign greatcoats** [*pokhodnyya shineli*] of the same color and pattern as the greatcoats of lower ranks, as described above for Grenadier regiments and following the same rules. With these greatcoats it is prescribed that there be worn swordbelts and pouchbelts of galloon in the same color as the buttons, but girdles are not to worn (Illus. 363) [296].

NOTES TO THE ILLUSTRATIONS
By Mark Conrad

327. By a decree of 1821 uniforms were as in the tables below. For officers, the braid, lace, monograms on the sabertache and saddle cloth - were all silver or gold, according to the color of the buttons. Slides on the girdle, or barrel sash, were silver, while the cords and tassels on the girdle, as well as shako cords, were silver mixed with black and orange silk. Officers' dolmans and pelisses had five rows of buttons, and the braid was laid on with the rows closely touching. Lower ranks had fifteen rows of braid and three rows of buttons.

Regiment.	Appointments.	Dolman.	Collar and cuffs of dolman and frock coat.	Pelisse.
Aleksandriya.	Silver.	Black.	Red.	Black.
Akhtyrka.	Gold.	Brown.	Yellow.	Brown.
Belorussia.	Silver.	Dark blue.	Red.	Red.
Grodno.	Silver.	Dark blue.	Sky blue.	Dark blue.

Regiment				
Yelisavetgrad.	Gold.	Grey.	Grey.	Grey.
Izyum.	Gold.	Red.	Dark blue.	Dark blue.
Irkutsk.	Gold.	Black.	Raspberry.	Black.
Lubny.	Silver.	Dark blue.	Yellow.	Dark blue.
Mariupol.	Gold.	Dark blue.	Yellow.	Dark blue.
Olviopol.	Silver.	Dark green.	Dark green.	Dark green.
Pavlograd.	Gold.	Dark green.	Turquoise.	Turquoise.
Sumy.	Silver.	Grey.	Red.	Grey.

As an exception, lower ranks in the Izyum Regiment had tinned buttons and chin scales.

Regiment.	*Chakchiry* pants.	Braid, galloon, and pompon.	Sabertache/trim.
Aleksandriya.	Black.	White.	Black/red.
Akhtyrka.	Dark blue.	Yellow.	Brown/yellow.
Belorussia.	Dark blue.	White.	Red/white.
Grodno.	Dark blue.	White.	Dark blue/sky blue.
Yelisavetgrad.	Dark green.	Red.	Dark green/red.
Izyum.	Dark blue.	White.	Red/white.
Irkutsk.	Raspberry.	Yellow.	Raspberry/yellow.
Lubny.	Dark blue.	White.	Dark blue/white.
Mariupol.	Dark blue.	Yellow.	Dark blue/yellow.
Olviopol.	Red.	White.	Dark green/red.
Pavlograd.	Dark green.	Red.	Dark green/red.
Sumy.	Red.	White.	Red/white.

Regiment.	Saddle cloth/trim/cord.	Girdle/slides.
Aleksandriya.	Black/red/white.	White/black.
Akhtyrka.	Dark blue/yellow/yellow.	Light blue/yellow.
Belorussia.	Red/white/white.	Red/white.
Grodno.	Dark blue/light blue/white.	Dark blue/white.
Yelisavetgrad.	Dark green/red/red.	Red/grey.
Izyum.	Red/white/white.	Dark blue/white.
Irkutsk.	Black/raspberry/yellow.	Yellow/black.
Lubny.	Dark blue/white/white.	Dark blue/white.
Mariupol.	Dark blue/yellow/yellow.	Dark blue/yellow.
Olviopol.	Dark green/red/white.	Red/white.
Pavlograd.	Dark green/red/red.	Red/turquoise.
Sumy.	Grey/red/white.	White/red.

328. Black leather reinforcement on the inside of the pants legs.

331. Thanks to some photographs of a special Imperial hand-colored edition of Viskovatov in Russia, taken by Mr. Rob Thomas of Milwaukee, Wisconsin, some notes on colors are possible. Here the turquoise distinguishing color is a light blue with a hint of grey. The sabertache slings are red leather; the valise is blue grey.

332. The inside of the shako is red. The grey distinguishing color of this regiment has a touch of blue.

333. The star on the shako has no shield in back of it. A mistake by the artist?

335. The back of the sabertache is black.

338. The yellow of the cap band here appears as a dirty yellow shade. The band has white piping on top and bottom.

346. The non-commissioned officer is mounted on a grey horse; there is white tape surrounding the rows of braid on the dolman. The yellow shakos of this regiment are a kind of darkish yellow, like a dirty orange shade, and the dark green is very dark, almost black.

348. The sabertache is described in the text as white with light-blue trim and monogram, but the plate shows these colors reversed.

352. The top of the shako is black. The light blue for this regiment is not very light, with a touch of grey.

353. The jacket on the right appears a slightly dark shade of reddish brown, and this officer's shako is a slightly dirty yellow.

354. The braid on these *vengerki*, as well as on the jackets of Illus. 353, appears to have small stripes of combined orange and black.

356. Yellow chevrons on the sleeve. The red of the dolman is a dull brick red, and not bright red or scarlet.

NOTES

(1) Collection of Laws and Regulations, 1826, Book I, pp. 108-110.

(2) Ibid., Book II, pg. 75.

(3) Ibid., Book III, pg. 255.

(4) Ibid., 1827, Book I, pg. 3.

(5) Ibid., Book III, pg. 89.

(6) Information received from the Commissariat Department of the War Ministry.

(7) Collection of Laws and Regulations, 1827, Book IV, pp. 17-19.

(8) Ibid., pp. 157-159.

(9) Ibid., pg. 257.

(10) Ibid., 1828, Book I, pg. 131, and Highest confirmed patterns preserved at the Commissariat Department of the War Ministry.

(11) Collection of Laws and Regulations, 1828, Book I, pg. 183, and information received from the Commissariat Department of the War Ministry.

(12) Collection of Laws and Regulations, 1828, Book II, pp. 131 et seq.

(13) Ibid., Book IV, pg. 47.

(14) Ibid., 1829, Book III, pg. 129.

(15) Ibid., Book IV, pg. 107.

(16) Ibid.

(17) Highest Order.

(18) Ibid.

(19) Collection of Laws and Regulations, 1830, Book III, pg. 217.

(20) Ibid., 1832, Book I, pg. 3.

(21) Ibid., Book III, pg. 329.

(22) Ibid., 1833, Book I, pg. 419.

(23) Ibid., pg. 435.

(24) Ibid., pg. 465.

(25) Ibid., pg. 485.

(26) Ibid., pg. 487.

(27) Ibid., pp. 234, 235, 300-307.

(28) Ibid., Book II, pg. 35.

(29) From correspondence of the Commissariat Department of the War Ministry.

(30) Information received from this same Department.

(31) Collection of Laws and Regulations, 1833, Book IV, pp. 121-125.

(32) Ibid., 1834, Book I, pg. 5.

(33) Ibid., Book II, pg. 233.

(34) Ibid., pg. 237.

(35) Ibid., pp. 245-247.

(36) Ibid., pg. 287-290.

(37) Ibid., pg. 209.

(38) Ibid., Book IV, pg. 141.

(39) Ibid., pg. 257.

(40) Ibid., 1835, Book I, pg. 137.

(41) Ibid., pg. 117.

(42) Ibid., pg. 367.

(43) Ibid., Book II, pg. 383.

(44) Ibid., Book III, pp. 175-178.

(45) Ibid., Book IV, pg. 55.

(46) Ibid., 1836, Book I, pp. 137 and 139.

(47) Ibid., Book II, pg. 171.

(48) Ibid., 1836, Book II, pg. 173.

(49) Collection of Laws and Regulations,.pg. 209.

(50) Ibid., Book IV, pp. 153 and 154.

(51) Ibid., 1837, Book I, pg. 133.

(52) Ibid., pg. 55.

(53) Ibid., pg. 123.

(54) Ibid., Book III, pg. 47.

(55) Ibid., Book IV, pg. 325.

(56) Ibid., 1838, Book I, pp. 311-315.

(57) Ibid., pg. 329.

(58) Ibid., pp. 337-340.

(59) Ibid., Book II, pg. 25.

(60) Ibid., 1839, Book I, pg. 3.

(61) Order of the Minister of War, 16 October 1840, № 71.

(62) ----------------------- 23 January 1841, № 8.

(63) Archive of the Inspection Department of the War Ministry, correspondence for 1842, Sect. 2 for the 2nd Office, № 365.

(64) Order of the Minister of War, 31 January 1843, № 16.

(65) ----------------------- 8 April 1843, № 44.

(66) ----------------------- 8 April 1843, № № 46 and 47.

(67) ----------------------- 8 April 1843, № № 46 and 47.

(68) ----------------------- 10 May 1843, №№ 63 and 64.

(69) ----------------------- 2 June 1843, № 78.

(70) ----------------------- 2 January 1844, № 1.

(71) ----------------------- 19 February 1844, № 16.

(72) ----------------------- 9 May 1844, №№ 63 and 64.

(73) ----------------------- 20 May 1844, № 69, pp. 8 and 9.

(74) ----------------------- 21 September 1844, № 8.

(75) ----------------------- 4 January 1845, № 1.

(76) ----------------------- 15 November 1845, № 139.

(77) ----------------------- 19 November 1845, № 140.

(78) ----------------------- 13 September 1846, № 160.

(79) Description of forage caps for lower ranks, appended to an order of the Minister of War, 19 May 1854 [sic, should be 1847? - M.C.], № 86.

(80) Report of the Director of the War Ministry to His Imperial Highness, the Commander-in-Chief of the Guards and Grenadier Corps, 7 July 1847, № 6,147.

(81) Order of the Minister of War, 31 August 1847, № 145.

(82) Report of the Minister of War to His Imperial Highness, the Commander-in-Chief of the Guards and Grenadier Corps, 5 November 1847, № 10,047.

(83) Ibid., 17 November 1847, № 10,478.

(84) Order of the Minister of War, 9 January 1848, № 8.

(85) ----------------------- 19 January 1848, № 17.

(86) ----------------------- 24 January 1848, № 22.

(87) ----------------------- 20 February 1848, № 36.

(88) ----------------------- 25 April 1848, № 80.

(89) ----------------------- 24 December 1849, № 133.

(90) ----------------------- 5 March 1850, № 18.

(91) ----------------------- 30 March 1851, № 36.

(92) ----------------------- 15 April 1851, № 48.

(93) ----------------------- 3 January 1852, № 2.

(94) ----------------------- 16 July 1852, № 81.

(95) ----------------------- 29 September 1852, № 107.

(96) ----------------------- 18 February 1854, № 21.

(97) Order of the Minister of War, 29 April 1854, № 53.

(98) Highest Order of 10 October 1854.

(99) Collection of Laws and Regulations, 1826, Book I, pp. 108-110.

(100) Ibid., Book II, pg. 75.

(101) Ibid., Book III, pg. 255.

(102) Ibid., 1827, Book I, pg. 3.

(103) Ibid., Book III, pg. 89.

(104) Ibid., Book IV, pp. 17-19.

(105) Ibid., pg. 257.

(106) Ibid., 1828, Book I, pg. 131.

(107) Ibid., pg. 183, and information received from the Commissariat Department of the War Ministry.

(108) Collection of Laws and Regulations, 1828, Book I, pg. 211.

(109) Ibid., Book II, pp. 131 et seq.
(110) Ibid., Book IV, pg. 47.
(111) Ibid., 1829, Book IV, pg. 107.
(112) Ibid., 1830, Book III, pg. 217.
(113) Ibid., 1832, Book I, pg. 3.
(114) Ibid., 1833, Book I, pg. 419.
(115) Ibid., pg. 435.
(116) Ibid., pg. 465.
(117) Ibid., pg. 485.
(118) Chronicle of the Russian IMPERIAL Army, Pt. V, 1852 ed.
(119) Collection of Laws and Regulations relating to the Military Administration, 1826, Book I, pp. 108-110.
(120) Ibid., Book II, pg. 75, and correspondence of the Commissariat Department of the War Ministry.
(121) Collection of Laws and Regulations, 1826, Book III, pg. 255.
(122) Ibid., 1827, Book I, pg. 3.
(123) Ibid., pg. 245.
(124) Ibid., Book II, pg. 147.
(125) Ibid., Book III, pg. 89.
(126) From correspondence of the Commissariat Department of the War Ministry.
(127) Collection of Laws and Regulations, 1827, Book IV, pp. 17-19.
(128) Ibid., pg. 257, and from correspondence of the Commissariat Department of the War Ministry.
(129) Ibid., 1828, Book I, pg. 105.
(130) Ibid., pg. 183, and from correspondence of the Commissariat Department of the War Ministry.
(131) Collection of Laws and Regulations, 1828, Book I, pg. 211.
(132) Ibid., Book IV, pg. 47.
(133) Ibid., pg. 83.
(134) Ibid., 1829, Book IV, pg. 107.
(135) Ibid., pg. 115.
(136) Highest Order.
(137) From correspondence of the Commissariat Department of the War Ministry.
(138) Collection of Laws and Regulations, 1830, Book III, pg. 217.
(139) Ibid., Book IV, pg. 401.
(140) Highest Order.
(141) Collection of Laws and Regulations, 1831, Book IV, pg. 141.
(142) Ibid., pg. 161, and from correspondence of the Commissariat Department of the War Ministry.
(143) Collection of Laws and Regulations, 1833, Book I, pg. 419.
(144) Ibid., pg. 435.
(145) Ibid., pp. 251-253.
(146) Collection of Laws and Regulations, pp. 284-335.
(147) From correspondence of the Inspection and Commissariat Departments of the War Ministry.
(148) From correspondence of the Commissariat Department of the War Ministry.
(148) Collection of Laws and Regulations, 1833, Book IV, pp. 121-125.
(149) Ibid., 1834, Book II, pg. 237.
(150) Collection of Laws and Regulations, 1834, Book II, pp.
245-247.
(151) Ibid., Book IV, pg. 141.
(152) Ibid., 1835, Book I, pg. 137.
(153) Ibid., pg. 317.
(154) From correspondence of the Commissariat Department of the War Ministry.
(155) Collection of Laws and Regulations, 1835, Book III, pg. 171.
(156) Ibid., pp. 175-178.
(157) Ibid., Book IV, pg. 35.
(158) Ibid., 1836, Book I, pg. 137.
(159) Ibid., Book IV, pg. 171.
(160) Ibid., pg. 209.
(161) Ibid., Book IV, pg. 153.
(162) Ibid., 1837, Book I, pg. 133.
(163) Ibid., 1837, Book I, pg. 55.
(164) Ibid., pg. 123.
(165) Ibid., Book III, pg. 89.
(166) Ibid., pg. 47.
(167) Ibid., pg. 65.
(168) Ibid., 1838, Book I, pg. 471.
(169) Ibid., 1837, Book IV, pg. 47.
(170) Ibid., 1833 [sic, should be 1838 - M.C.], Book I, pp. 311-315.
(171) Ibid., pg. 329.
(172) Ibid., pg. 61.
(173) Ibid., Book II, pg. 26.
(174) Ibid., 1839, Book I, pg. 3.
(175) Order of the Minister of War, 16 October 1840, № 71.
(176) ----------------------------- 23 January 1841, № 8.
(177) ----------------------------- 31 January 1843, № 16.
(178) ----------------------------- 8 April 1843, №№ 44 and 46.
(179) ----------------------------- 10 May 1843, №№ 62 and 64.
(180) ----------------------------- 17 September 1843, No 117.
(181) ----------------------------- 2 January 1844, № 1.
(182) ----------------------------- 19 February 1844, № 16.
(183) ----------------------------- 20 May 1844, № 69, pp. 10 and 11.
(184) ----------------------------- 21 September 1844, № 115.
(185) ----------------------------- 15 November 1845, № 139.
(186) ----------------------------- 19 November 1845, № 140.
(187) ----------------------------- 13 September 1846, № 160.
(188) Memorandum of the Duty General of HIS IMPERIAL MAJESTY'S Main Staff to the Inspector of Reserve Cavalry, 28 December 1846, №11902.
(189) Description of forage caps for lower ranks, appended to an order of the Minister of War, 19 May 1854 [sic, should be 1847? - M.C.], № 86.
(190) Report of the Director of the War Ministry to His Imperial Highness, the Commander-in-Chief of the Guards and Grenadier Corps, 7 July 1847, № 6,147.
(191) Highest Order of 29 September 1847 and information received at the Commissariat Department of the War Ministry.
(192) Order of the Minister of War, 19 January 1848, № 17.
(193) ----------------------------- 25 April 1848, № 80.
(194) ----------------------------- 7 November 1849, № 111.
(195) ----------------------------- 24 December 1849, № 133.
(196) ----------------------------- 5 March 1850, № 18.
(197) ----------------------------- 3 February 1851, № 12.

(198) ----------------------------- 30 March 1851, № 36.

(199) ----------------------------- 15 April 1851, № 48.

(200) ----------------------------- 31 December 1851, № 140 § 12.

(201) ----------------------------- 3 January 1852, № 2.

(202) ----------------------------- 18 January 1852, № 11.

(203) ----------------------------- 21 February 1852, № 26.

(204) ----------------------------- 16 July 1852, № 81.

(205) ----------------------------- 13 August 1853, № 61.

(206) ----------------------------- 18 February 1854, № 21.

(207) ----------------------------- 29 April 1854, № 53.

(208) Collection of Laws and Regulations, 1826, Book I, pp. 108-110.

(209) Ibid., Book II, pg. 75.

(210) Ibid., Book III, pg. 255.

(211) Information received from the Commissariat Department of the War Ministry.

(212) Collection of Laws and Regulations, 1827, Book I, pg. 3.

(213) Ibid., Book I, pg. 155.

(214) Ibid., Book III, pg. 75.

(215) Ibid., pg. 89.

(216) Ibid., Book IV, pp. 17-19.

(217) Ibid., pg. 255.

(218) Ibid., pg. 257.

(219) Ibid., 1828, Book I, pg. 163.

(220) Ibid., pg. 183.

(221) Ibid., Book I, pg. 211.

(222) Ibid., Book II, pp. 131 et seq.

(223) Ibid., Book IV, pg. 33.

(224) Ibid., pg. 47.

(225) Ibid., 1829, Book IV, pg. 107.

(226) Ibid., 1830, Book II, pg. 97.

(227) Ibid., Book III, pg. 217.

(228) Ibid., 1832, Book I, pg. 3.

(229) Ibid., Book IV, pg. 127.

(230) Ibid., 1833, Book I, pg. 419.

(231) Ibid., pg. 435.

(232) Ibid., pp. 465.

(233) Ibid., pp. 309, 313, 317, 321, 325, 329, and 333.

(234) From correspondence of the Commissariat Departments of the War Ministry.

(235) Collection of Laws and Regulations, 1834, Book I, pp. 203-207.

(236) Ibid., Book II, pg. 237.

(237) Ibid., pp. 245-247.

(238) Ibid., Book IV, pg. 141.

(239) Ibid., pg. 257.

(240) Ibid., 1835, Book I, pg. 337.

(241) Ibid., pg. 117.

(242) Ibid., pg. 367.

(243) Ibid., Book II, pg. 283.

(244) Information received from the Commissariat Departments of the War Ministry.

(245) Collection of Laws and Regulations, 1835, Book III, pp. 175-178, and memorandum from the Commander of the L.-Gds. Hussar Regiment, 6 November 1846, № 2241.

(246) Collection of Laws and Regulations, 1836, Book I, pg. 137.

(247) Ibid., Book II, pg. 171.

(248) Ibid., pg. 209.

(249) Ibid., Book IV, pg. 153.

(250) Ibid., 1837, Book I, pg. 55.

(251) Ibid., pg. 123.

(252) Ibid., Book IV, pg. 325.

(253) Collection of Laws and Regulations, 1838, Book I, pg. 329.

(254) Ibid., Book II, pg. 423.

(255) Ibid., 1839, Book I, pg. 3.

(256) Ibid., Book I, pg. 31.

(257) Order of the Minister of War, 16 October 1840, № 71.

(258) ----------------------------- 23 January 1841, № 8.

(259) ----------------------------- 8 April 1843, №№ 46 and 47.

(260) ----------------------------- 8 April 1843, №№ 46 and 47.

(261) ----------------------------- 10 May 1843, №№ 63 and 64.

(262) ----------------------------- 2 June 1843, № 78.

(263) ----------------------------- 2 January 1844, № 1.

(264) ----------------------------- 19 February 1844, № 16.

(265) ----------------------------- 20 May 1844, № 69, pp. 10 and 11.

(266) ----------------------------- 21 September 1844, № 115.

(267) ----------------------------- 17 December 1844, № 155.

(268) ----------------------------- 10 January 1845, № 8.

(269) ----------------------------- 26 February 1845, № 35.

(270) ----------------------------- 18 August 1845, № 106.

(271) ----------------------------- 8 September 1845, № 111.

(272) ----------------------------- 15 November 1845, № 139.

(273) ----------------------------- 13 September 1846, № 160.

(274) Memorandum of the Commissariat Department to the Inspection Department of the War Ministry, 26 October 1846, № 8572.

(275) Description of lower ranks' forage caps, appended to an order of the Minister of War, 19 May 1854 [sic, should be 1847 - M.C.], № 86.

(276) Report of the Director of the War Ministry to His Imperial Highness, the Commander-in-Chief of the Guards and Grenadier Corps, 7 July 1847, № 6,147.

(277) Order of the Minister of War, 19 January 1848, № 17.

(278) ----------------------------- 25 April 1848, № 80.

(279) ----------------------------- 7 November 1849, № 111.

(280) ----------------------------- 17 December 1849, № 130.

(281) ----------------------------- 24 December 1849, № 133.

(282) ----------------------------- 5 March 1850, № 18.

(283) ----------------------------- 10 June 1850, № 44.

(284) ----------------------------- 30 March 1851, № 36.

(285) ----------------------------- 15 April 1851, № 48.

(286) ----------------------------- 3 January 1852, № 2.

(287) ----------------------------- 14 June 1852, № 67.

(288) ----------------------------- 12 July 1852, № 76.

(289) ----------------------------- 16 July 1852, № 81.

(290) ----------------------------- 29 August 1852, № 97.

(291) ----------------------------- 3 January 1853, № 3.

(292) ----------------------------- 13 August 1853, № 61.

(293) ----------------------------- 27 November 1853, № 81.

(294) ----------------------------- 11 February 1854, № 15.

(295) ----------------------------- 18 February 1854, № 21.

(296) ----------------------------- 29 April 1854, № 53.

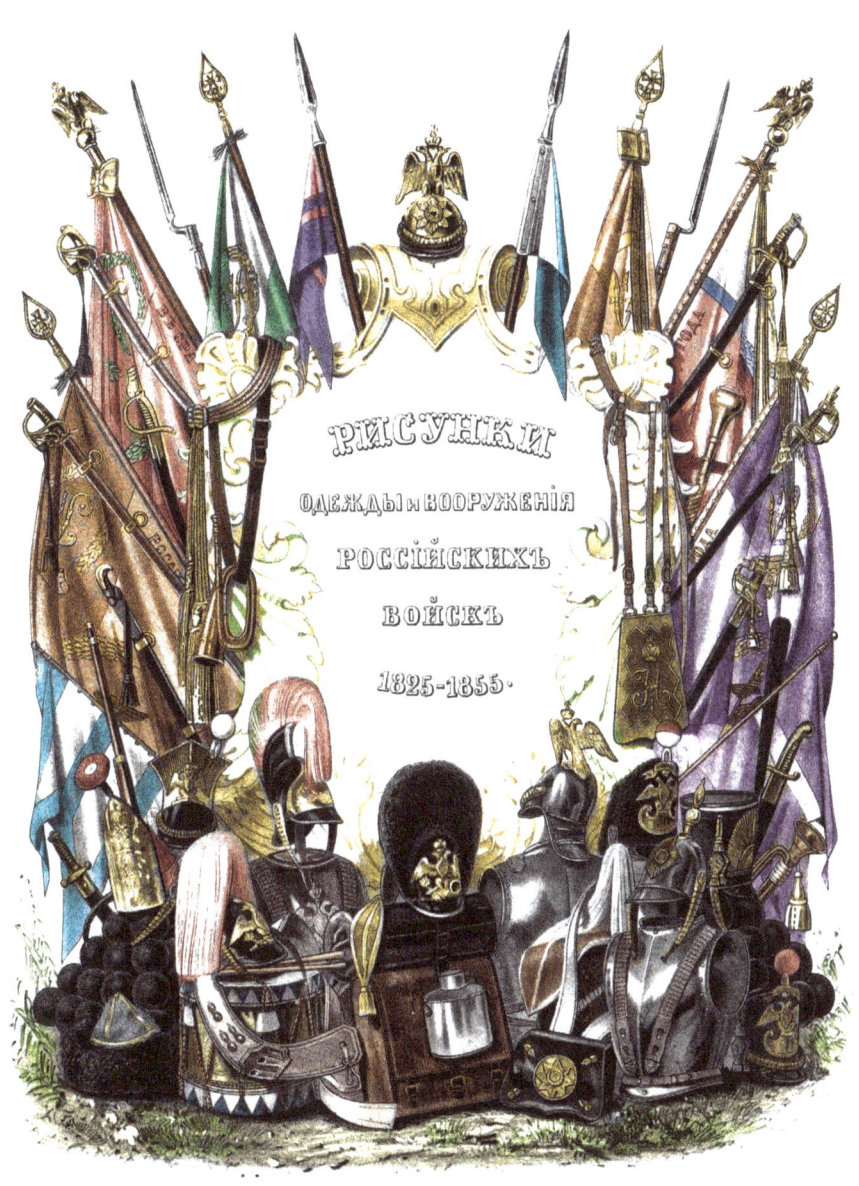

РИСУНКИ

ОДЕЖДЫ и ВООРУЖЕНІЯ

РОССІЙСКИХЪ

ВОЙСКЪ

1825-1855.

PLATES LIST OF ILLUSTRATIONS

261. Musket case for Dragoon regiments, confirmed 17 November 1847.

262. Private. His imperial Highness the Heir and Tsesarevich's Dragoon Regiment. 1848-1855.

263. Field-grade Officer. New Russia Dragoon Regiment. 1848-1852.

264. Bandolier for standards in Dragoon regiments, established 5 March 1850.

265. Private. Prince Emile of Hesse's Dragoon Regiment. 1851-1855.

266. Firing-pin cover for Cavalry percussion weapons, established 3 January and 16 July, 1852.

267. Company-grade Officer. His imperial Highness the Grand Duke Michael Nikolaevich's Dragoon Reg. 1852-1855.

268. Field-grade Officer. Riga Dragoon Regiment. 1854 and 1855.

269. Company-grade Officer. His Royal Highness the Crown Prince of Württemberg's Dragoon Regiment. 1854 and 1855.

270. Privates. Severskii and Chernigov Horse-Jäger Regiments. 1826 and 1827.

271. Non-commissioned Officers. Nezhin and Dorpat Horse-Jäger Regiments. 1826 and 1827.

272. Staff-trumpeters. Pereyaslavl and His Majesty the King of Württemberg's Horse-Jäger Regiments. 1826 and 1827.

273. Officer of the Arzamas Horse-Jäger Reg. and Company-grade Officer of the Tiraspol Horse-Jäger Reg.. 1826 and 1827.

274. Private and Company-grade Officer. Severskii Horse-Jäger Regiment. 1827 and 1828.

275. Private and Company-grade Officer. Chernigov Horse-Jäger Regiment. 1828.

276. Company-grade Officer of the Dorpat Horse-Jäger Reg. and Private of the Tiraspol Horse-Jäger Reg. 1828-1833.

277. Private. Belgorod Lancer Regiment. 1826-1828.

278. Non-commissioned Officer. Chuguev Lancer Regiment. 1826-1828.

279. Trumpeter. Borisoglebsk Lancer Regiment. 1826-1828.

280. Company-grade Officer. Serpukhov Lancer Regiment. 1826-1828.

281. NCO of the 1st Bug Lancer Regiment and Company-grade Officer of the 2nd Bug Lancer Regiment. 1826-1828.

282. Privates. 3rd and 4th Bug Lancer Regiments. 1826-1828.

283. Staff-trumpeter of the 1st Ukraine Lancer Reg. and NCO of the 2nd Ukraine Lancer Regiment. 1826-1828.

284. Field-grade Officer of the 3rd Ukraine Lancer Reg. and Officer of the 4th Ukraine Lancer Reg.. 1826-1828.

285. Privates. His imperial Highness the Grand Duke Michael Nikolaevich's and the Siberia Lancer Reg. 1827 and 1828.

286. NCO of the Orenburg Lancer Regiment and Trumpeter of the Yamburg Lancer Regiment. 1827 and 1828.

287. Company-grade Officer. His imperial Highness the Grand Duke Michael Nikolaievich's Lancer Reg.. 1827 and 1828.

288. Private. St.-Petersburg Lancer Regiment. 1827 and 1828.

289. Non-commissioned Officer. Kharkov Lancer Regiment. 1827 and 1828.

290. Trumpeter of the Smolensk Lancer Reg. and Company-grade Officer of the Courland Lancer Reg. 1827 and 1828.

291. Field-grade Officer. Polish Lancer Regiment. 1827 and 1828.

292. Private. St.-Petersburg Lancer Regiment. 1828-1833.

293. Company-grade Officer. Siberia Lancer Regiment. 1829-1833.

294. Trumpeter of the Bug Lancer Regiment and Company-grade Officer of the Odessa Lancer Regiment. 1830-1833.

295. Private of the Voznesensk Lancer Regiment and NCO of the Olviopol Lancer Regiment. 1830-1833.

296. Privates. Polish and Tatar Lancer Regiments. 1830 and 1831.

297. Non-commissioned Officers. Lithuania and Volhynia Lancer Regiments. 1830-1833.

298. Field-grade Officer. Polish Lancer Regiment. 1831-1833.

299. Private. St.-Petersburg Lancer Regiment. 1833.

300. Private. Courland Lancer Regiment. 1833.

301. Non-commissioned Officers. Smolensk and Kharkov Lancer Regiments. 1833.

302. Trumpeters. Lithuania and Volhynia Lancer Regiments. 1833.

303. Company-grade Officers. Orenburg and Siberia Lancer Regiments. 1833.

304. Field-grade Officers. Voznesensk and Olviopol Lancer Regiments. 1833.

305. Private of the Bug Lancer Regiment and Non-commissioned Officer of the Odessa Lancer Regiment. 1833.

306. Company-grade Officer of His imperial Highness the Grand Duke Michael Nikolaievich's Lancer Regiment and Trumpeter of the Yamburg Lancer Regiment. 1833.

307. Privates. Belgorod and Chuguev Lancer Regiments. 1833.

308. Non-commissioned Officers. Borisoglebsk and Serpukhov Lancer Regiments. 1833.

309. Staff-trumpeter of the Ukraine Lancer Regiment and Private of the Novo-Arkhangelsk Lancer Regiment. 1833.

310. Company-grade Officer. Novo-Mirgorod Lancer Regiment. 1833.

311. Field-grade Officer. Yelisavetgrad Lancer Regiment. 1833.

312. Staff-Trumpeter. Ukraine Lancer Regiment. 1836-1855.

313. Kettledrum banner of the St.-Petersburg Lancer Regiment, confirmed 17 August 1837.

314. Company-grade Officer. His imperial Highness heir and Tsesarecich's Lancer Regiment. 1838-1855.

315. Non-commissioned Officer. Voznesensk Lancer Regiment. 1843-1855.

316. Field-grade Officer. His imperial Highness the Grand Duke Nicholas Aleksandrovich's Lancer Regiment. 1843-1852.

317. Company-grade Officer. Her imperial Highness the Grand Duchess Catherine Mikailonma's Lancer Reg. 1846-1855.

318. Field-grade Officer. His imperial Highness the Grand Duke Constantine Nikolaievich's Lancer Regiment. 1847-1855.

319. Private. His imperial Highness the Grand Duke Nicholas Aleksandrovich's Lancer Regiment. 1852-1855.

320. Non-commissioned Officer. Bug Lancer Regiment. 1852-1855.

321. Field-grade Officer. His Highness Archduke Carl Ferdinand of Austria's Lancer Regiment. 1852-1855.

322. Private. Archduke Leopold of Austria's Lancer Regiment. 1852-1855.

323. Non-commissioned Officer. Novo-Arkhangelsk Lancer Regiment. 1852-1855.

324. Company-grade Officer. Novo-Mirgorod Lancer Regiment. 1852-1855.

325. Field-grade Officer. Her imperial Highness the Grand Duchess Catherine Mikailovna's Lancer Regiment. 1852-1855.

326. Company-grade Officer. His imperial Highness the Heir and Tsesarevich's Lancer Regiment. 1854 and 1855.

327. Private. Sumy Hussar Regiment. 1826-1828.

328. Non-commissioned Officer. Olviopol Hussar Regiment. 1826-1828.

329. Trumpeter of the Klyastitsy Hussar Regiment and Staff-trumpeter of the Lubny Hussar Regiment. 1826-1828.

330. Company-grade Officer and Non-commissioned Officer. Archduke Ferdinand's Hussar Regiment. 1826-1828.

331. Company-grade Officer. Pavlograd Hussar Regiment. 1826-1828.

332. Company-grade Officer and Field-grade Officer. Yelisavetgrad Hussar Regiment. 1826-1828.

333. Company-grade Officer and Private. Irkutsk Hussar Regiment. 1826-1828.

334. Privates. Akhtyrka, Aleksandriya, and Graf Wittgenstein's Hussar Regiments. 1826-1828.

335. Non-commissioned Officers. The Prince of Orange's, the Ingermanland, and the Narva Hussar Regiments. 1826-1828.

336. Trumpeter of the Kiev Hussar Regiment and Company-grade Officer of the Mitau Hussar Regiment. 1826-1828.

337. Hussar officers' girdle, established 17 February 1827.

338. Private. Lubny Hussar Regiment. 1827 and 1828.

339. Company-grade Officers. The Prince of Orange's and Archduke Ferdinand's Hussar Regiments. 1827-1830.

340. Privates. Archduke Ferdinand's Hussar Regiment. 1828-1844.

341. Company-grade Officer of the Sumy Hussar Regiment and Private of the Olviopol Hussar Regiment. 1828-1833.

342. Company-grade Officer. Sumy Hussar Regiment. 1830-1833.

343. Field-grade Officer. His imperial Highness the Grand Duke Michael Pavolovich's Hussar Regiment. 1832 and 1833.

344. Non-commissioned Officer. Akhtyrka Hussar Regiment. 1833.

345. Private, Non-commissioned Officer, and Field-grade Officer. Kiev Hussar Regiment. 1834 and 1835.

346. NCO and Company-grade Officer. His Majesty the King of Württemberg's Hussar Regiment. 1834 and 1835.

347. Trumpeter. Kiev Hussar Regiment. 1836-1838.

348. Private and Field-grade Officer. Klyastitsy Hussar Regiment. 1833-1843.

349. Private. Archduke Ferdinand's Hussar Regiment. From 1843 on.

350. Hussar shoulder cords showing rank, established 8 April 1843.

351. Officers' shoulder cords for showing rank in Hussar regiments, established 17 December 1844.

352. Officer and Private. Her imperial Highness the Grand Duchess Olga Nikolaevna's Hussar Regiment. 1845-1855.

353. Company-grade Officers. His imperial Highness Duke Maximilian of Leuchtenberg's and General-Adjutant Prince Vasilchikov's Hussar Regiments. 1845-1855. (In jackets.)

354. Company-grade Officers. Her imperial Highness the Grand Duchess Olga Nikolaevna's and the Klyastitsy Hussar Regiments. 1845-1855. (In *vengerka* coats.)

355. Private of the Klyastitsy Hussar Regiment and Company-grade Officer of His imperial Highness the Heir and Tsesarevich's Hussar Regiment. 1849-1855.

356. Non-commissioned Officer. Archduke Ferdinand's Hussar Regiment. 1850-1855.

357. Private. Prince Frederick-Carl of Prussia's Hussar Regiment. 1851-1855.

358. Field-grade Officer. His Royal Highness Prince Frederick-Carl's Hussar Regiment. 1852-1855.

359. Private. General-Adjutant Graf von-der-Pahlen's Hussar Regiment. 1853-1855.

360. Company-grade Officer. General-Adjutant Graf von-der-Pahlen's Hussar Regiment. 1853-1855.

361. Private. General-Adjutant Graf von-der-Pahlen's Hussar Regiment. 1853-1855.

362. Company-grade Officers. General-Adjutant Graf von-der-Pahlen's Hussar Regiment. 1853-1855.

363. Company-grade Officer. Her imperial Highness the Grand Duchess Olga Nikolaevna's Hussar Reg. 1854 and 1855.

Privates. L.Gds Preobrazhenskii, Semenovskii, and Izmailovskii Regiments, 1802-1805

Non-commissioned Officer of the Kinburn Dragoon Regiment and Private of the New Russia Dragoon Regiment. 1826 and 1827

Trumpeter and Staff-trumpeter. Kazan and Riga Dragoon Regiments. 1826 and 1827

Company-grade Officers. Tver and Finland Dragoon Regiments. 1826 and 1827

Field-grade Officers. St.-Petersburg and Kharkov Dragoon Regiments. 1826 and 1827.

Company-grade Officers. Smolensk and Courland Dragoon Regiments. 1826 and 1827

Privates. Ingermanland and Narva Dragoon Regiments. 1826 and 1827

Non-commissioned Officer of the Kiev Dragoon Regiment and Trumpeter of the Mitau Dragoon Regiment. 1826 and 1827

Field-grade Officer. Nizhnii-Novgorod Dragoon Regiment. 1827 and 1828

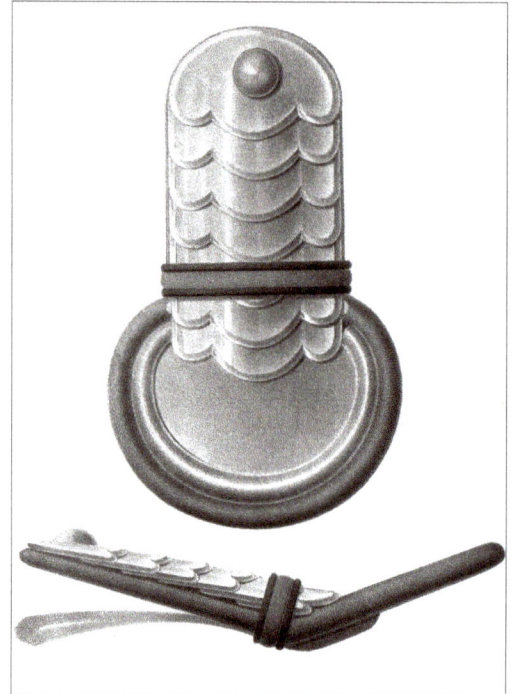

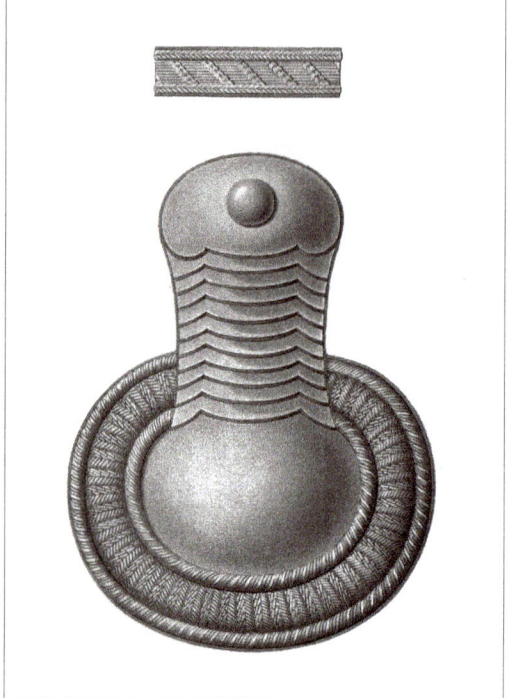

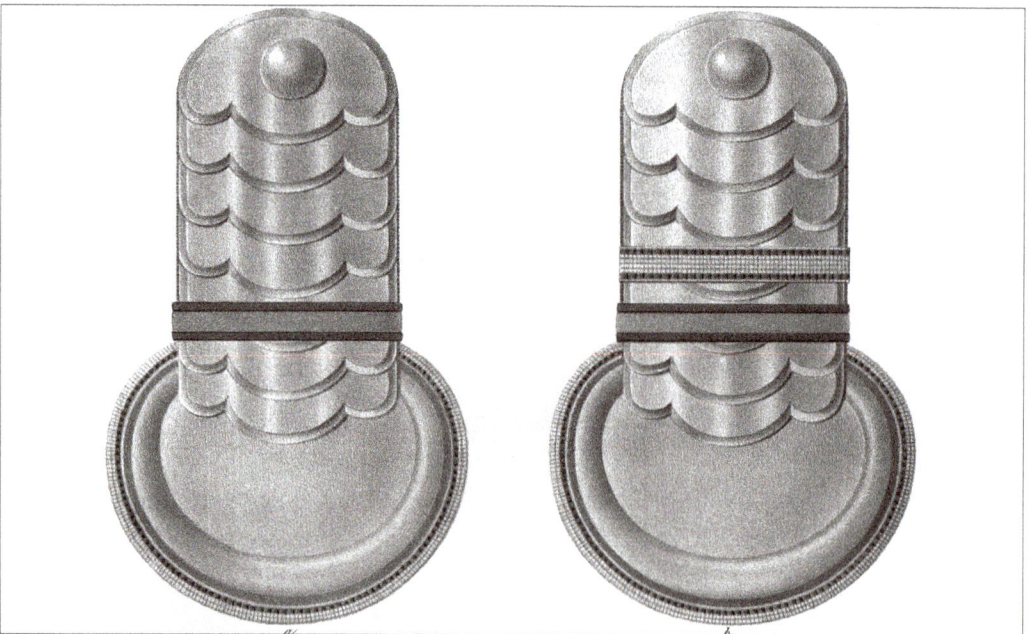

Lower ranks' Épaulette for Dragoon Regiments, confirmed 13 October 1827. - Officers' Épaulette for Dragoon Regiments, confirmed 13 October 1827.

Lower ranks' epaulettes for Dragoon Regiments, confirmed 7 May 1828

Private of the Moscow Dragoon Regiment and Company-grade Officer of the Kargopol Dragoon Regiment. 1827 and 1828

Non-commissioned Officers. Kinburn, New Russia, and Kazan Dragoon Regiments. 1827 and 1828

Privates. His Royal Highness Duke Alexander of Württemberg's, Tver, Finland, and New Russia Dragoon Regiments. 1827 and 1828

Dragoon Shako, confirmed 9 February 1828

Private and Non-commissioned Officer. Kinburn Dragoon Regiment. 1828

Company-grade Officer. New Russia Dragoon Regiment. 1828

Private. Kazan Dragoon Regiment. 1828-1833

Private and Company-grade Officer. Nizhnii-Novgorod Dragoon Regiment. 1829-1834

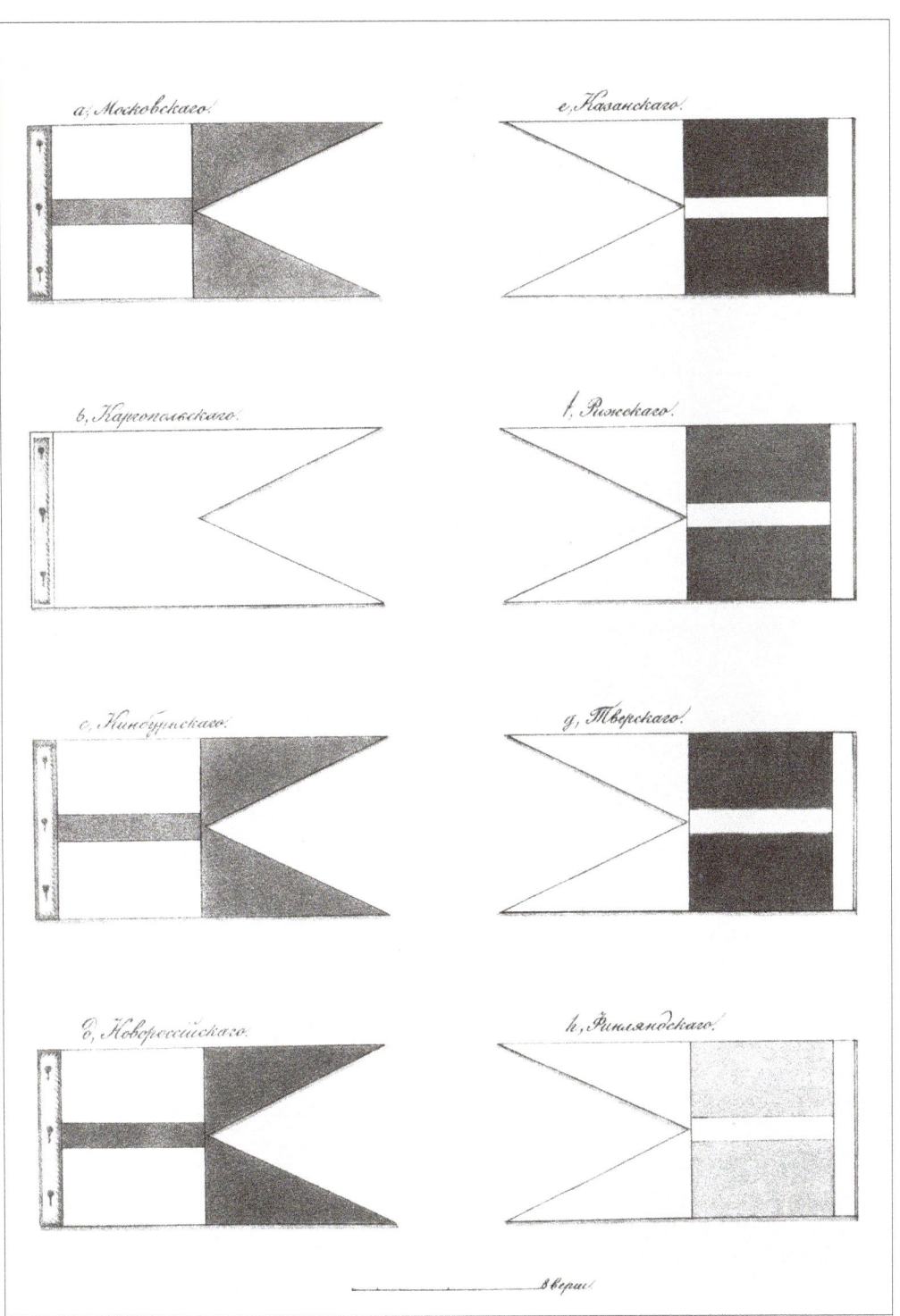

a, Московскаго.

b, Каргопольскаго.

c, Кинбурнскаго.

d, Новороссійскаго.

e, Казанскаго.

f, Рижскаго.

g, Тверскаго.

h, Финляндскаго.

Pennons for Dragoon regiments, confirmed 20 April 1833

Private of the Moscow Dragoon Regiment and Non-commissioned Officer of the Kargopol Dragoon Regiment. 1833-1843

Private. Kinburn Dragoon Regiment. 1833-1843

Company-grade Officer and Private. New Russia Dragoon Regiment. 1833-1836.

238

Non-commissioned Officers. Kazan and Riga Dragoon Regiments. 1833-1843

63

Trumpeter of the Tver Dragoon Regiment and Private of the Finland Dragoon Regiment. 1833-1834

Private. Kinburn Dragoon Regiment. 1834-1843

Company-grade Officer and Private. Nizhnii-Novgorod Dragoon Regiment. 1834-1836.

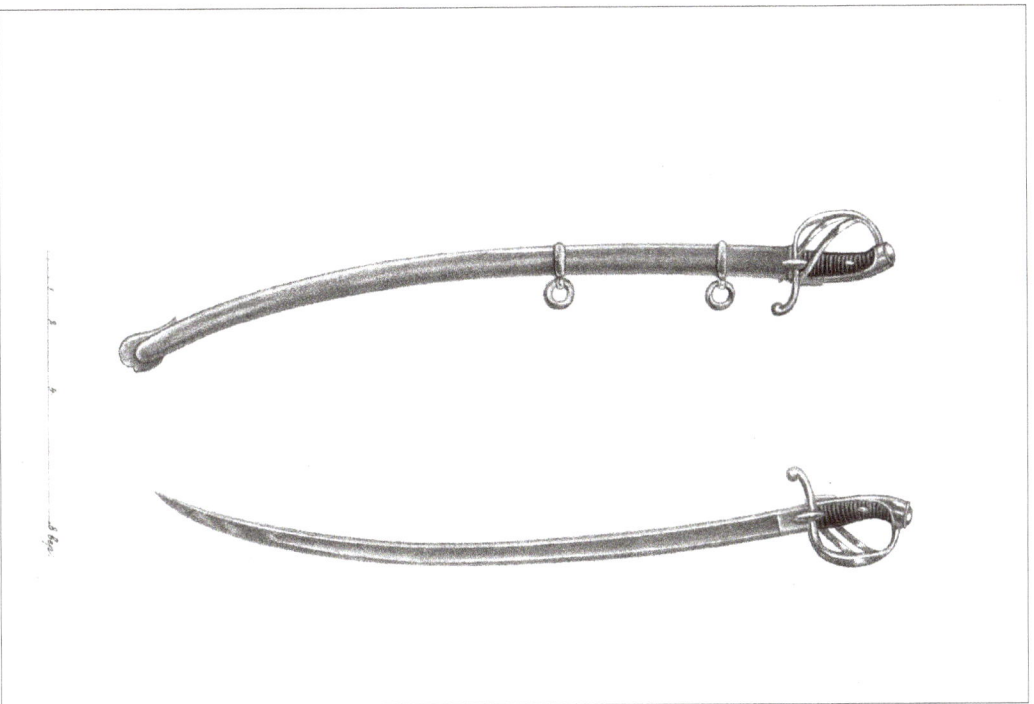

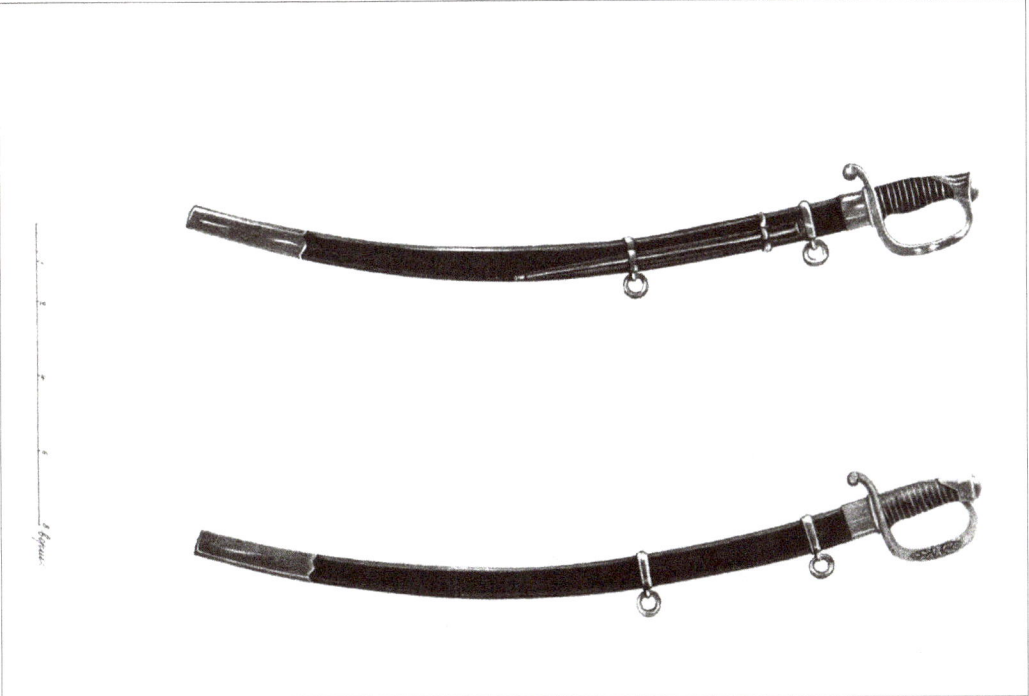

Dragoon Saber, confirmed 8 October 1827 - Dragoon Sabers, confirmed 13 November 1841

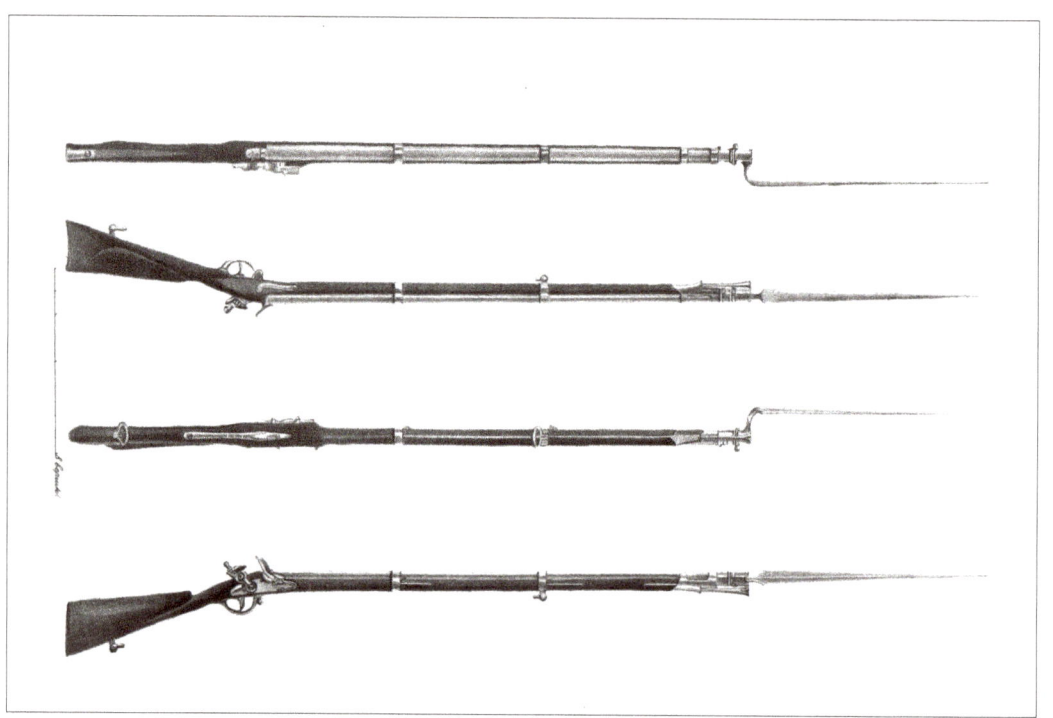

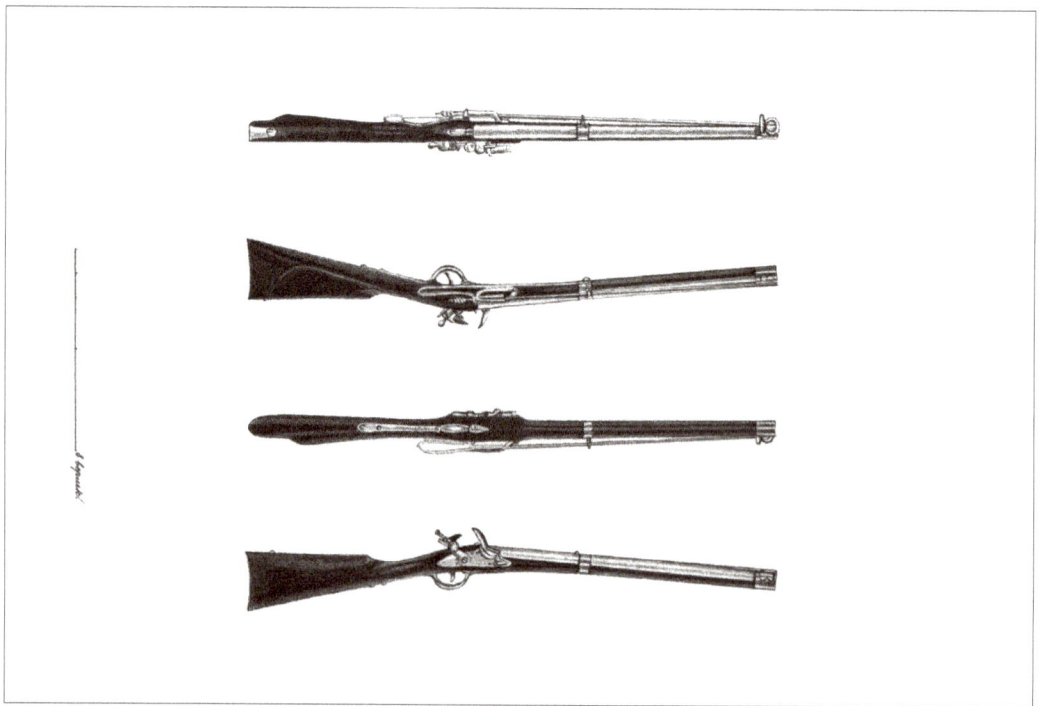

Dragoon musket, confirmed 30 June 1834 - Carbine, confirmed 11 March 1837

Private. Kazan Dragoon Regiment. 1834-1843

Company-grade Officers. Riga Dragoon Regiment. 1835-1843

Private. Nizhnii-Novgorod Dragoon Regiment. From 1836.

Shapka headdresses for lower ranks of the Nizhnii-Novgorod Dragoon Regiment, confirmed 31 January 1836

Trumpeter. Moscow Dragoon Regiment. 1836-1845

Drummer. Moscow Dragoon Regiment. 1836-1841

Officers' epaulette for Dragoon regiments, confirmed 11 December 1837.

Company-grade Officers. His imperial Dragoon Regiments. 1838-1844

253

Private. His Royal Highness Prince Alexander of the Netherlands' Dragoon Regiment. 1843-1844

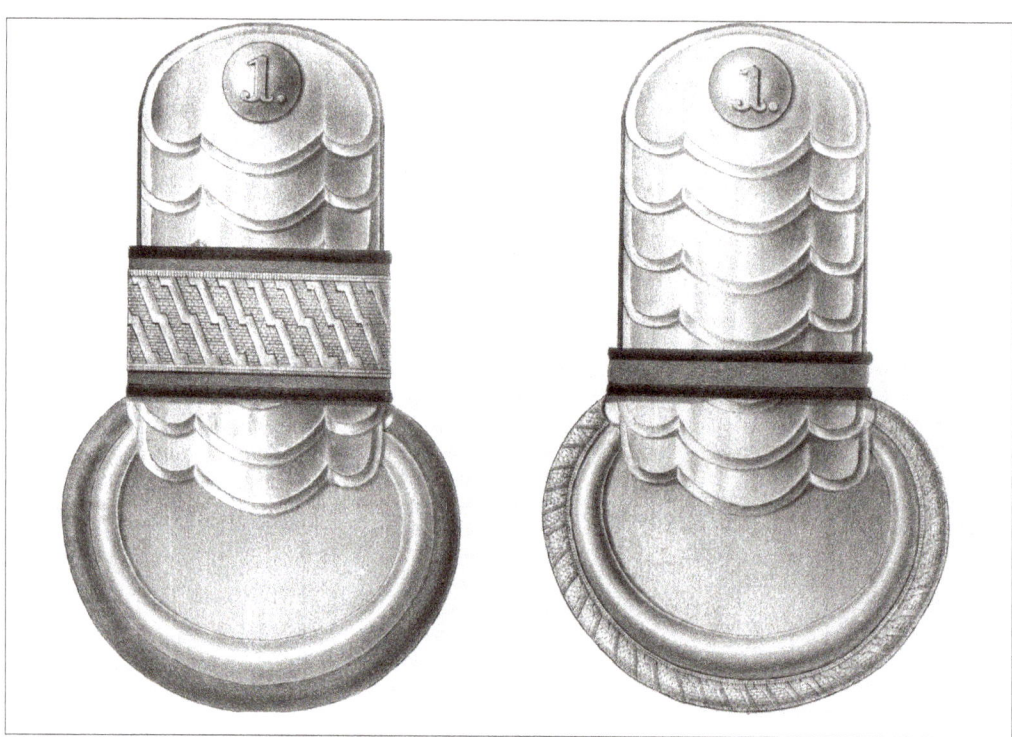

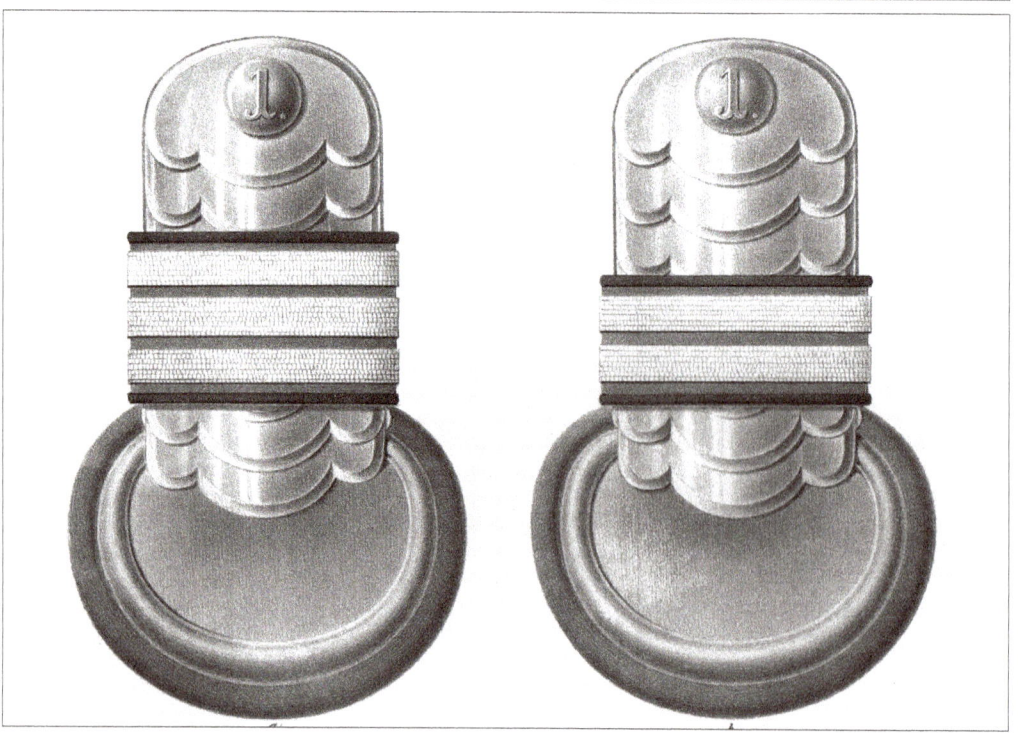

Lower ranks' epaulettes of Dragoon regiments, with rank distinctions, confirmed 8 April 1843

Lance-corporals' epaulette for Dragoon regiments, confirmed 8 April 1843.

Trumpeter and Non-commissioned Officer. His Majesty Prince Emile of Hesse's Dragoon Regiment. 1844-1848

Company-grade Officer. Riga Dragoon Regiment. 1845-1848

Private. His imperial Dragoon Regiment. 1847-1855

Private. His imperial Dragoon Regiment. 1847 and 1848

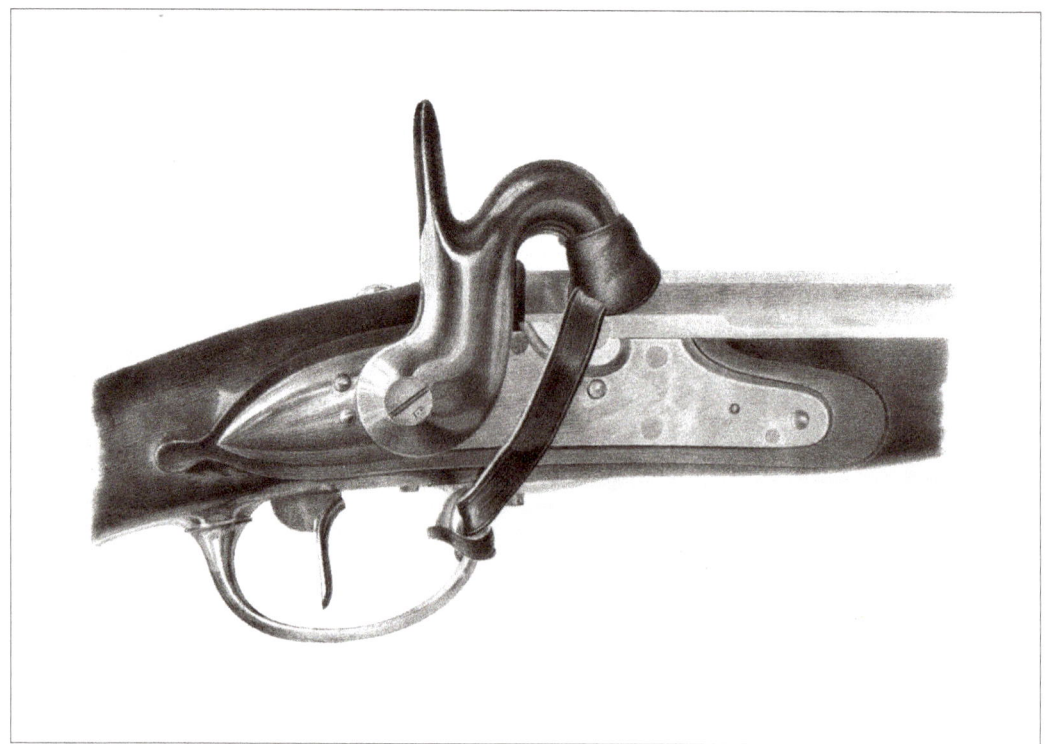

Musket case for Dragoon regiments, confirmed 17 November 1847

Firing-pin cover for Cavalry percussion weapons, established 3 January and 16 July, 1852

262

Private. His imperial Dragoon Regiment. 1848-1855

Field-grade Officer. New Russia Dragoon Regiment. 1848-1852

Private. Prince Emile of Hesse's Dragoon Regiment. 1851-1855

Company-grade Officer. His imperial Dragoon Regiment. 1852-1855

Field-grade Officer. Riga Dragoon Regiment. 1854 and 1855.

Company-grade Officer. His Royal Highness the Crown Prince of Württemberg's Dragoon Regiment. 1854 and 1855

Privates. Severskii and Chernigov Horse-Jäger Regiments. 1826 and 1827

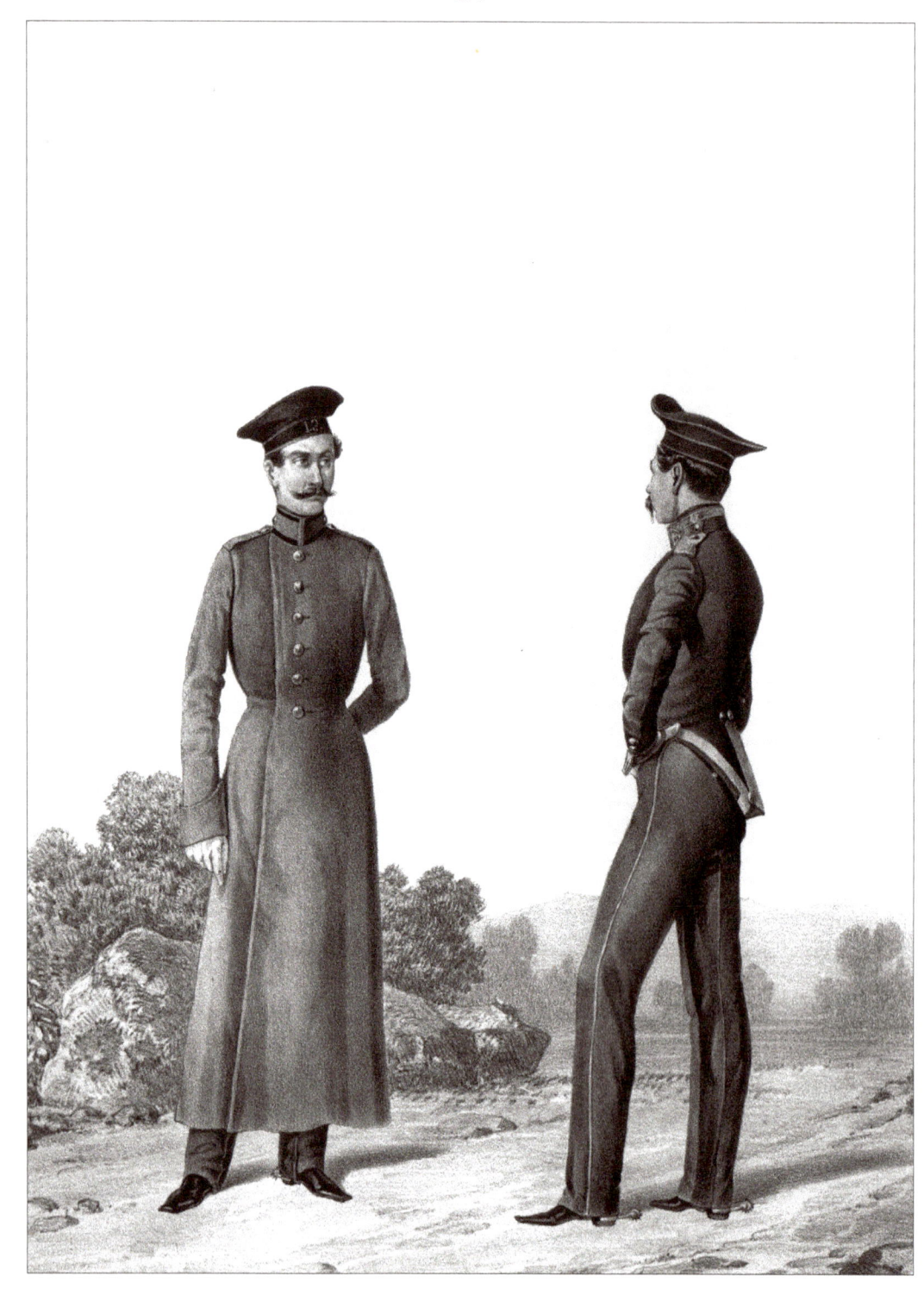

Non-commissioned Officers. Nezhin and Dorpat Horse-Jäger Regiments. 1826 and 1827

Staff-trumpeters. Pereyaslavl and His Majesty the King of Württemberg's Horse-Jäger Regiments. 1826 and 1827

Field-grade Officer of the Arzamas Horse-Jäger Regiment and Company-grade Officer of the Tiraspol Horse-Jäger Regiment. 1826 and 1827

Private and Company-grade Officer. Severskii Horse-Jäger Regiment. 1827 and 1828.

Private and Company-grade Officer. Chernigov Horse-Jäger Regiment. 1828

Company-grade Officer of the Dorpat Horse-Jäger Regiment and Private of the Tiraspol Horse-Jäger Regiment. 1828-1833

Private. Belgorod Lancer Regiment. 1826-1828

Non-commissioned Officer. Chuguev Lancer Regiment. 1826-1828

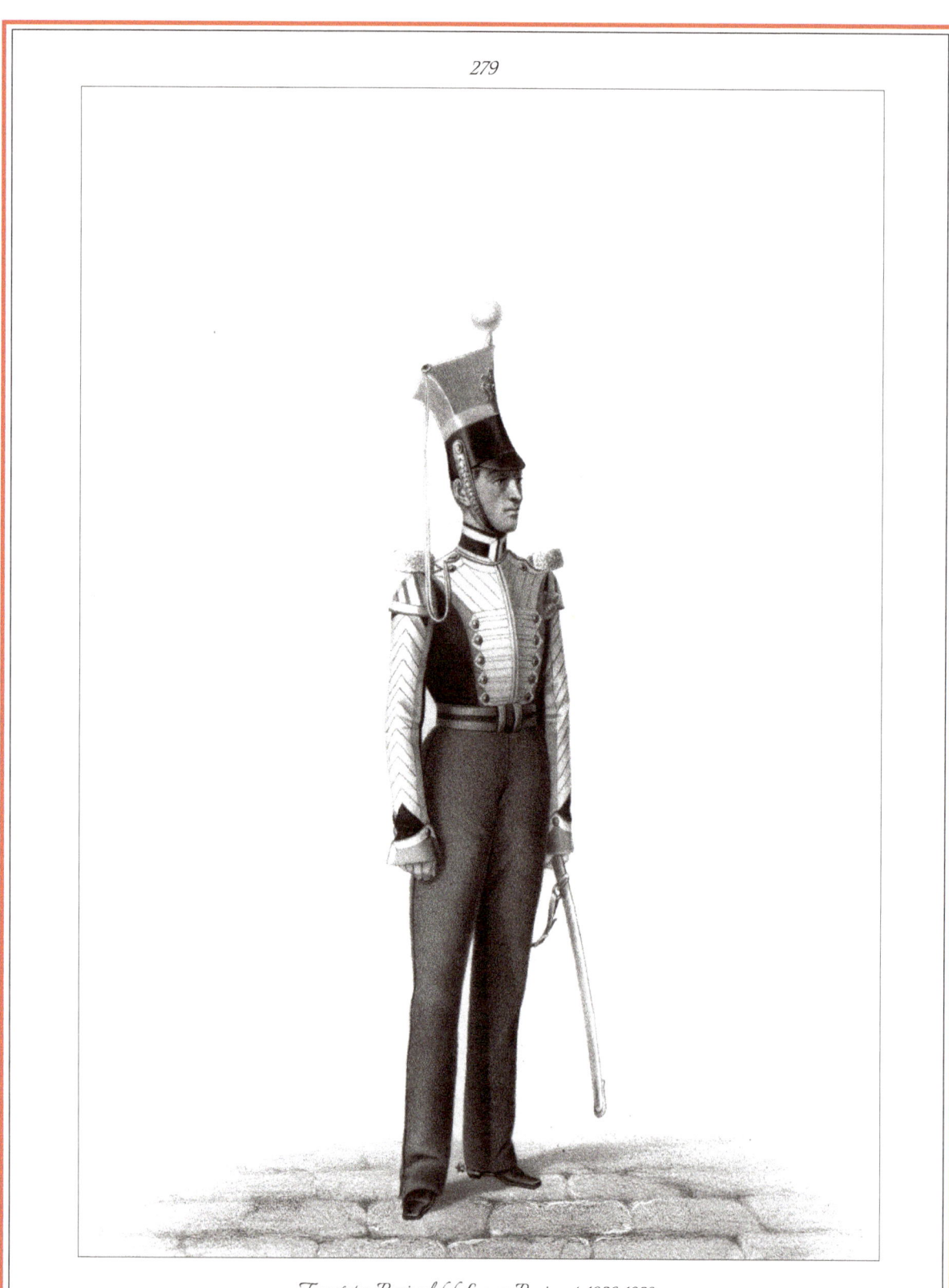

Trumpeter. Borisoglebsk Lancer Regiment. 1826-1828

Company-grade Officer. Serpukhov Lancer Regiment. 1826-1828

Non-commissioned Officer of the 1st Bug Lancer Regiment and Company-grade Officer of the 2nd Bug Lancer Regiment. 1826-1828

Privates. 3rd and 4th Bug Lancer Regiments. 1826-1828

Staff-trumpeter of the 1st Ukraine Lancer Regiment and Non-commissioned Officer of the 2nd Ukraine Lancer Regiment. 1826-1828

Field-grade Officer of the 3rd Ukraine Lancer Regiment and Company-grade Officer of the 4th Ukraine Lancer Regiment. 1826-1828

Privates. His imperial and the Siberia Lancer Regiments. 1827 and 1828

Non-commissioned Officer of the Orenburg Lancer Regiment and Trumpeter of the Yamburg Lancer Regiment. 1827 and 1828

Company-grade Officer. His imperial Lancer Regiment. 1827 and 1828

Private. St.-Petersburg Lancer Regiment. 1827 and 1828.

Non-commissioned Officer. Kharkov Lancer Regiment. 1827 and 1828

Trumpeter of the Smolensk Lancer Regiment and Company-grade Officer of the Courland Lancer Regiment. 1827 and 1828

Field-grade Officer. Polish Lancer Regiment. 1827 and 1828

Private. St.-Petersburg Lancer Regiment. 1828-1833

Company-grade Officer. Siberia Lancer Regiment. 1829-1833

Trumpeter of the Bug Lancer Regiment and Company-grade Officer of the Odessa Lancer Regiment. 1830-1833

Private of the Voznesensk Lancer Regiment and Non-commissioned Officer of the Olviopol Lancer Regiment. 1830-1833

Privates. Polish and Tatar Lancer Regiments. 1830 and 1831

Non-commissioned Officers. Lithuania and Volhynia Lancer Regiments. 1830-1833

Field-grade Officer. Polish Lancer Regiment. 1831-1833

Private. St.-Petersburg Lancer Regiment. 1833.

Private. Courland Lancer Regiment. 1833

Non-commissioned Officers. Smolensk and Kharkov Lancer Regiments. 1833

Trumpeters. Lithuania and Volhynia Lancer Regiments. 1833

Company-grade Officers. Orenburg and Siberia Lancer Regiments. 1833

Field-grade Officers. Voznesensk and Olviopol Lancer Regiments. 1833

Private of the Bug Lancer Regiment and Non-commissioned Officer of the Odessa Lancer Regiment. 1833

Company-grade Officer of his imperial Lancer Regiment and Trumpeter of the Yamburg Lancer Regiment. 1833

Privates. Belgorod and Chuguev Lancer Regiments. 1833

Non-commissioned Officers. Borisoglebsk and Serpukhov Lancer Regiments. 1833

Staff-trumpeter of the Ukraine Lancer Regiment and Private of the Novo-Arkhangelsk Lancer Regiment. 1833

Company-grade Officer. Novo-Mirgorod Lancer Regiment. 1833

Field-grade Officer. Yelisavetgrad Lancer Regiment. 1833

Staff-Trumpeter. Ukraine Lancer Regiment. 1836-1855.

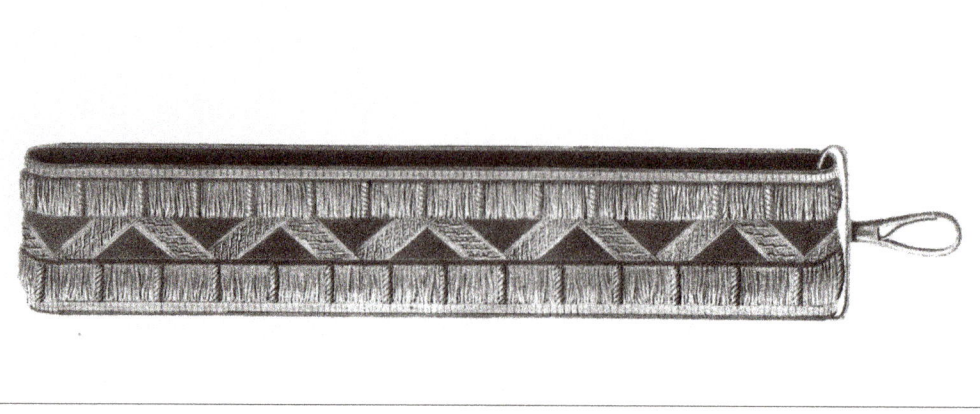

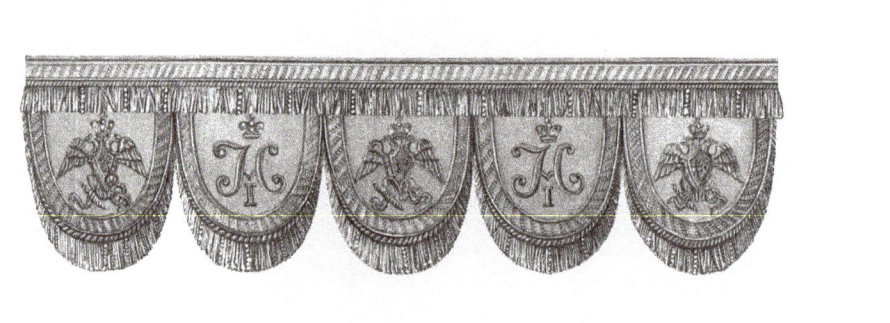

Bandolier for standards in Dragoon regiments, established 5 March 1850
Kettledrum banner of the St.-Petersburg Lancer Regiment, confirmed 17 August 1837
Hussar officers' girdle, established 17 February 1827

Company-grade Officer. His imperial Lancer Regiment. 1838-1855

Non-commissioned Officer. Voznesensk Lancer Regiment. 1843-1855

Field-grade Officer. His imperial Lancer Regiment. 1843-1852

Company-grade Officer. Her imperial Catherine Mikhailovna's Lancer Regiment. 1846-1855

Field-grade Officer. his imperial Constantine Nikolaevich's Lancer Regiment. 1847-1855

Private. His imperial Nickolas Alexandrovich's Lancer Regiment. 1852-1855

Non-commissioned Officer. Bug Lancer Regiment. 1852-1855

Field-grade Officer. His Highness Archduke Carl Ferdinand of Austria's Lancer Regiment. 1852-1855

Private. Archduke Leopold of Austria's Lancer Regiment. 1852-1855

Non-commissioned Officer. Novo-Arkhangelsk Lancer Regiment. 1852-1855

Company-grade Officer. Novo-Mirgorod Lancer Regiment. 1852-1855

Field-grade Officer. Her imperial Catherine Mikhailovna's Lancer Regiment. 1852-1855

Company-grade Officer. His imperial Lancer Regiment. 1854 and 1855

Private. Sumy Hussar Regiment. 1826-1828

Non-commissioned Officer. Olviopol Hussar Regiment. 1826-1828

Trumpeter of the Klyastitsy Hussar Regiment and Staff-trumpeter of the Lubny Hussar Regiment. 1826-1828

Company-grade Officer and Non-commissioned Officer. Archduke Ferdinand's Hussar Regiment. 1826-1828

Company-grade Officer. Pavlograd Hussar Regiment. 1826-1828

Company-grade Officer and Field-grade Officer. Yelisavetgrad Hussar Regiment. 1826-1828

334

Company-grade Officer and Private. Irkutsk Hussar Regiment. 1826-1828

Privates. Akhtyrka, Aleksandriya, and Graf Wittgenstein's Hussar Regiments. 1826-1828

Non-commissioned Officers. The Prince of Orange's, the Ingermanland, and the Narva Hussar Regiments. 1826-1828

Trumpeter of the Kiev Hussar Regiment and Company-grade Officer of the Mitau Hussar Regiment. 1826-1828

Private. Lubny Hussar Regiment. 1827 and 1828

Company-grade Officers. The Prince of Orange's and Archduke Ferdinand's Hussar Regiments. 1827-1830

Privates. Archduke Ferdinand's Hussar Regiment. 1828-1844

Company-grade Officer of the Sumy Hussar Regiment and Private of the Olviopol Hussar Regiment. 1828-1833

Company-grade Officer. Sumy Hussar Regiment. 1830-1833

Field-grade Officer. His imperial Hussar Regiment. 1832 and 1833

344

Non-commissioned Officer. Akhtyrka Hussar Regiment. 1833

Private, Non-commissioned Officer, and Field-grade Officer. Kiev Hussar Regiment. 1834 and 1835

Non-commissioned Officer and Company-grade Officer. His Majesty the King of Württemberg's Hussar Regiment. 1834 and 1835

Trumpeter. Kiev Hussar Regiment. 1836-1838

Private and Field-grade Officer. Klyastitsy Hussar Regiment. 1833-1843

Private. Archduke Ferdinand's Hussar Regiment. From 1843 on

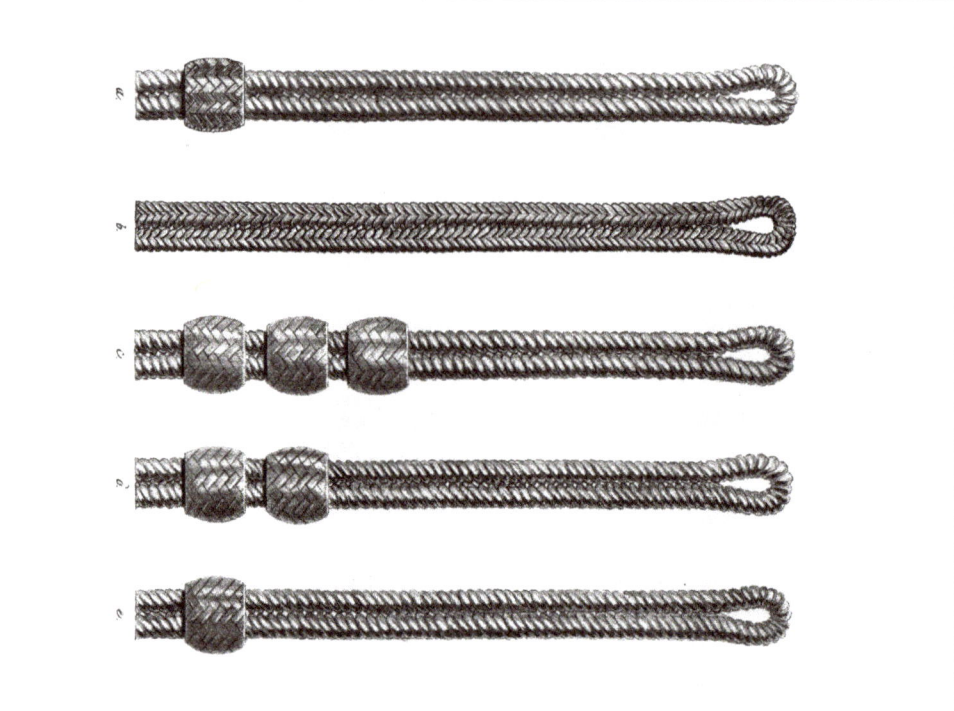

Hussar shoulder cords showing rank, established 8 April 1843 - Officers' shoulder cords for showing rank in Hussar regiments, established 17 December 1844

Company-grade Officer and Private. Her imperial Hussar Regiment. 1845-1855

353

Company-grade Officers. His imperial and General-Adjutant Prince Vasilchikov's Hussar Regiments. 1845-1855. (In jackets.)

Company-grade Officers. Her imperial and the Klyastitsy Hussar Regiments. 1845-1855. (In vengerka coats.)

Private of the Klyastitsy Hussar Regiment and Company-grade Officer of his imperial Hussar Regiment. 1849-1855

Non-commissioned Officer. Archduke Ferdinand's Hussar Regiment. 1850-1855

Private. Prince Frederick-Carl of Prussia's Hussar Regiment. 1851-1855

Field-grade Officer. His Royal Highness Prince Frederick-Carl's Hussar Regiment. 1852-1855

Private. General-Adjutant Graf von-der-Pahlen's Hussar Regiment. 1853-1855

Company-grade Officer. General-Adjutant Graf von-der-Pahlen's Hussar Regiment. 1853-1855

Private. General-Adjutant Graf von-der-Pahlen's Hussar Regiment. 1853-1855

Company-grade Officers. General-Adjutant Graf von-der-Pahlen's Hussar Regiment. 1853-1855

Company-grade Officer. Her imperial Hussar Regiment. 1854 and 1855

SOLDIERS, WEAPONS & UNIFORMS ALREADY PUBLISHED
(SOME TITLES)

UNIFORMS OF RUSSIAN ARMY IN THE ERA OF ANCIENT TZAR
FROM THE REIGN OF VASILI IV TO MICHAEL I, ALEXIS, FEODOR III DURING THE XVII th CENTURY
A.V.VISKOVATOV — LUCA STEFANO CRISTINI
SWU-600-004

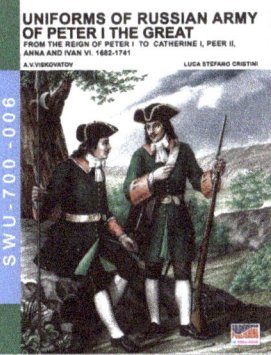

UNIFORMS OF RUSSIAN ARMY OF PETER I THE GREAT
FROM THE REIGN OF PETER I TO CATHERINE I, PEER II, ANNA AND IVAN VI. 1682-1741
A.V.VISKOVATOV — LUCA STEFANO CRISTINI
SWU-700-006

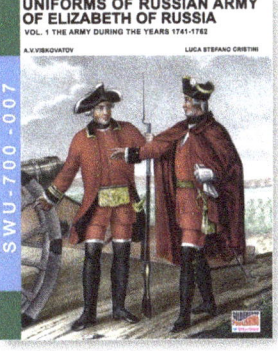

UNIFORMS OF RUSSIAN ARMY OF ELIZABETH OF RUSSIA
VOL.1 THE ARMY DURING THE YEARS 1741-1762
A.V.VISKOVATOV — LUCA STEFANO CRISTINI
SWU-700-007

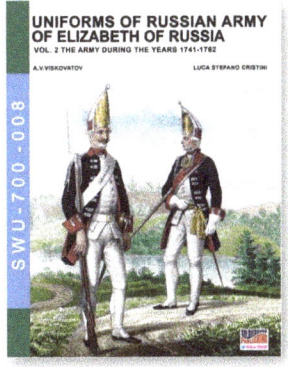

UNIFORMS OF RUSSIAN ARMY OF ELIZABETH OF RUSSIA
VOL.2 THE ARMY DURING THE YEARS 1741-1762
A.V.VISKOVATOV — LUCA STEFANO CRISTINI
SWU-700-008

UNIFORMS OF RUSSIAN ARMY IN THE XVIII CENTURY VOL. 1
UNDER THE REIGN OF CATHERINE II EMPRESS OF RUSSIA BETWEEN 1762 AND 1796
A.V.VISKOVATOV - LUCA STEFANO CRISTINI
SWU-700-005

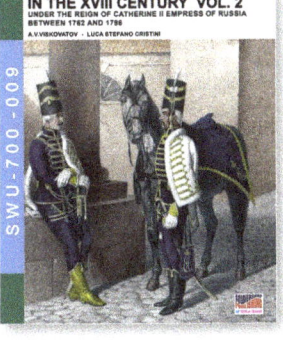

UNIFORMS OF RUSSIAN ARMY IN THE XVIII CENTURY VOL. 2
UNDER THE REIGN OF CATHERINE II EMPRESS OF RUSSIA BETWEEN 1762 AND 1796
A.V.VISKOVATOV - LUCA STEFANO CRISTINI
SWU-700-009

UNIFORMS OF RUSSIAN ARMY IN THE XVIII CENTURY VOL. 3
UNDER THE REIGN OF CATHERINE II EMPRESS OF RUSSIA BETWEEN 1762 AND 1796
A.V.VISKOVATOV - LUCA STEFANO CRISTINI
SWU-700-010

UNIFORMS OF RUSSIAN ARMY IN THE XVIII CENTURY VOL. 4
UNDER THE REIGN OF CATHERINE II EMPRESS OF RUSSIA BETWEEN 1762 AND 1796
A.V.VISKOVATOV - LUCA STEFANO CRISTINI
SWU-700-011

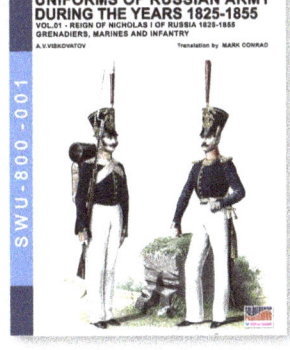

UNIFORMS OF RUSSIAN ARMY DURING THE YEARS 1825-1855
VOL.01 - REIGN OF NICHOLAS I OF RUSSIA 1825-1855 GRENADIERS, MARINES AND INFANTRY
A.V.VISKOVATOV   Translation by MARK CONRAD
SWU-800-001

UNIFORMS OF RUSSIAN ARMY DURING THE YEARS 1825-1855
VOL.02 - REIGN OF NICHOLAS I OF RUSSIA 1825-1855 CARABINIERS, JÄGERS, RIFLES, AND CUIRASSIERS
A.V.VISKOVATOV   Translation by MARK CONRAD
SWU-800-002

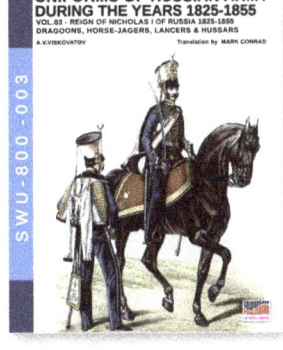

UNIFORMS OF RUSSIAN ARMY DURING THE YEARS 1825-1855
VOL.03 - REIGN OF NICHOLAS I OF RUSSIA 1825-1855 DRAGOONS, HORSE-JAGERS, LANCERS & HUSSARS
A.V.VISKOVATOV   Translation by MARK CONRAD
SWU-800-003

UNIFORMS OF RUSSIAN ARMY DURING THE YEARS 1825-1855
VOL.04 - REIGN OF NICHOLAS I OF RUSSIA 1825-1855 GENDARMES, TRAIN, ARTILLERY, SAPPERS & PIONEERS
A.V.VISKOVATOV   Translation by MARK CONRAD
SWU-800-004

UNIFORMS OF RUSSIAN ARMY DURING THE NAPOLEONIC WAR
VOL.5 - REIGN OF PAUL I 1796 AND 1801 - THE GUARDS 1
A.V.VISKOVATOV   TRANSLATION BY MARK CONRAD
EBOOK SWU-NAP-010

UNIFORMS OF RUSSIAN ARMY DURING THE NAPOLEONIC WAR
VOL.10 - REIGN OF ALEXANDER I OF RUSSIA 1801-1825 CAVALRY: CUIRASSIERS, DRAGOONS & HORSE-JÄGERS
A.V.VISKOVATOV   Translation by MARK CONRAD
SWU-NAP-015

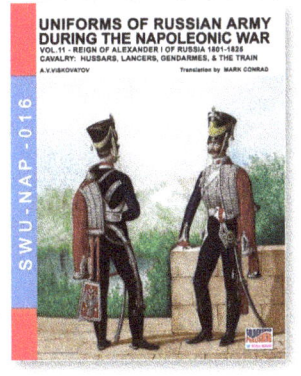

UNIFORMS OF RUSSIAN ARMY DURING THE NAPOLEONIC WAR
VOL.11 - REIGN OF ALEXANDER I OF RUSSIA 1801-1825 CAVALRY: HUSSARS, LANCERS, GENDARMES, & THE TRAIN
A.V.VISKOVATOV   Translation by MARK CONRAD
SWU-NAP-016

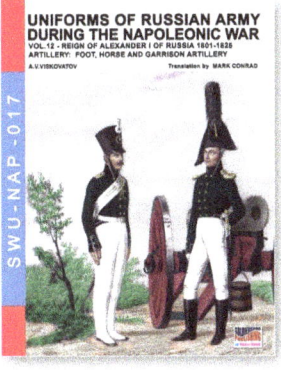

UNIFORMS OF RUSSIAN ARMY DURING THE NAPOLEONIC WAR
VOL.12 - REIGN OF ALEXANDER I OF RUSSIA 1801-1825 ARTILLERY: FOOT, HORSE AND GARRISON ARTILLERY
A.V.VISKOVATOV   Translation by MARK CONRAD
SWU-NAP-017